Studies of Unionism in Government

Managing
Local Government
under
Union Pressure

Studies of Unionism in Government

DAVID T. STANLEY
with the assistance of Carole L. Cooper

Managing Local Government under Union Pressure

THE BROOKINGS INSTITUTION
Washington, D.C.

HD
8008
S7
1972

132210

ISBN 0–8157–8102–4
Library of Congress Catalog Card Number 73–183218

9 8 7 6 5 4 3 2 1

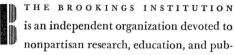

Foreword

Governmental institutions in the United States, burdened as never before with critical problems of public policy and with major difficulties in obtaining and allocating resources, are experiencing stress from another source: the pressures of public employee unionism. Recent years have seen an almost explosive growth in union membership, rapidly expanding use of collective bargaining, and more aggressive behavior, including a willingness to strike, by union leaders. These pressures have created unprecedented difficulties for the decision-making machinery of government.

To assist public and union officials and others who are associated with the collective bargaining process in government to make informed decisions, the Brookings Institution launched in 1967 a program of research on unionism in government at the state and local levels. This program was undertaken with the encouragement of the National Civil Service League and financial support from the Ford Foundation. The first product of this research program—and the first book in the Studies of Unionism in Government series—was *The Unions and the Cities,* by Harry H. Wellington and Ralph K. Winter, Jr., both of Yale Law School and members of the Brookings associated staff. That study treats both theoretical and practical problems of law, political science, and economics that result from the growing use of collective bargaining, with emphasis on the regulation of government–union relations.

The present book, the second in the Brookings series, discusses the effect union pressures are having on local government administration. Mayors, councils, city managers, and department heads have always been influenced in their decision making by the views of interested citizen groups. Now they are sharing more and more of their authority with organized employees as well. What this means for civil service systems, for pay-setting processes, for budget planning, and for decisions on manning and work-loads is explored here.

This study was made by David T. Stanley, senior fellow in the Governmental Studies Program and author of three earlier Brookings books on public personnel matters. Carole L. Cooper served as his research assistant throughout the project. Interviews in nine of the nineteen governments selected as research sites (fifteen cities and four urban counties) were conducted by Mr. Stanley and Miss Cooper. Six others—R. G. Beers, Barry Casper, W. Donald Heisel, Raymond D. Horton, Carleton F. Sharpe, and John W. Steele— also conducted interviews, and reviewed and commented on the manuscript.

The chief executives and staffs of the cities and counties visited were most helpful in providing information, as were officials of the unions concerned.

The authors are grateful also to the following persons for their assistance and counsel: Kenneth O. Warner and other staff members of the Public Personnel Association; Sam Zagoria and James Baird of the Labor-Management Relations Service of the National League of Cities, National Association of Counties, and U.S. Conference of Mayors; David B. Walker and other staff members of the Advisory Commission on Intergovernmental Relations; and the staffs of the International City Management Association and the Municipal Finance Officers Association. Thanks are also due to the principal researchers on the other studies in this series: Arnold R. Weber, Jack Stieber, Harry H. Wellington, Ralph K. Winter, Jr., John F. Burton, Jr., and Paul T. Hartman. At Brookings, Gilbert Y. Steiner, Director of Governmental Studies, and Allen Schick of the Governmental Studies staff commented on the manuscript.

Further acknowledgments for assistance are due to Charles Krider of the University of Chicago, Winston W. Crouch of the University of California at Los Angeles; Jean J. Couturier of the National Civil Service League; Jerry Wurf and Mary Lou Hennessy of the American Federation of State, County, and Municipal Employees; Frederick C. Mosher of the University of Virginia; Felix A. Nigro of the University of Georgia; Albert H. Aronson of the Office of State Merit Systems, U.S. Department of Health, Education, and Welfare; the late Harold S. Roberts and the staffs of the Industrial Relations Center and its Library at the University of Hawaii; and the staff of the Institute of Industrial Relations of the University of California (Berkeley).

Sara Sklar performed indispensable services as administrative assistant and secretary. Additional typing was done by Margie Barringer. Evelyn P. Fisher checked the manuscript for accuracy. The manuscript was edited by Virginia C. Haaga, and the index was prepared by Joan C. Culver.

The statements, conclusions, and recommendations in this book are those of the authors and do not necessarily reflect the views of staff members, officers, or trustees of the Brookings Institution or the Ford Foundation.

KERMIT GORDON
President

October 1971
Washington, D.C.

Contents

1. **Public Administration and Unions in Nineteen Local Governments**   1

What Is Public Administration? *4*
The Governments Studied *5*
State Laws on Collective Bargaining *10*
The Unions in the Cities and Counties *13*
Method of Study and Presentation *14*

2. **The Employment Relationship**   16

The Employment Bargain in Government *17*
Where Does Management Start? *20*
Management Rights *21*
Organization for Labor Relations *25*
The Tone of the Relationship *30*

3. **Effect on Hiring, Promotion, Training, and Grievances**   32

Hiring New Employees *32*
Promotions *36*
Employee Training *46*
Grievances and Discipline *50*
General Quality of Relations *58*

4. **Effect on Classification, Pay, and Benefits**   60

Position Classification *60*
Methods of Setting Pay *64*
How Large Were the Raises? *74*
Hours of Work *79*

Overtime and Other Special Pay Arrangements *80*
Fringe Benefits *82*
Conclusion *88*

5. *Effect on Work Management and Working Conditions*   89
Resistance to Contracting *90*
Workload, Manning, and Program Policy *93*
Work Assignments—When and Where? *101*
Whose Work? *105*
Working Conditions *107*
Conclusion *111*

6. *Effect on Budget and Finance*   112
The Fiscal Problem of Local Governments *113*
Putting the Budget Together *115*
Financing Difficulties *120*
Handing the Money to Departments *132*
Conclusion *135*

7. *The Impact in General: Present and Prospective*   136
Effect on Administration of Local Governments *138*
Effect on State Governments *142*
Are There Limits to Unions' Power in Administration? *143*
Administration in a Unionized Future *148*

Appendixes

A. Labor Relations Training Programs of the Cities of Detroit and Milwaukee *153*
B. Pay and Benefit Liberalizations in the Nineteen Local Governments Surveyed *156*
C. Provisions Relating to Working Conditions of the 1967 Contract between the New York City Department of Social Services and the Social Service Employees Union   *161*
D. Selected Bibliography *164*

Index   171

Tables

1. Population and Census Region of the Nineteen Local Governments Surveyed, 1960 *6*
2. Official with Primary Bargaining Responsibility in the Nineteen Local Governments Surveyed, 1969 *26*
3. Use of Negotiated Grievance Procedures and Arbitration in Resolving Contested Disciplinary Actions Taken by the Nineteen Local Governments Surveyed *57*

4. Pay Increases Granted by Those Governments among the Nineteen Surveyed That Did Not Use Collective Bargaining, Calendar Years 1968 and 1969 *76*

5. Pay Increases Granted by Those Governments among the Nineteen Surveyed That Used Collective Bargaining, Calendar Years 1968 and 1969 *76*

A-1. Labor Relations Training Programs of the Civil Service Commission of the City of Detroit, 1966–69 *153*

A-2. Labor Relations Training Programs of the City Service Commission of the City of Milwaukee, 1964–69 *154*

Public Administration and Unions in Nineteen Local Governments

Today's intractable and often-studied local government problems (law enforcement, air pollution, transportation, housing, health), are partly problems of government administration. Difficulties in personnel management, work planning, and budgeting contribute to the total difficulty of governing the deeply troubled cities of the United States. To state it more positively, effective administration can help upgrade the quality of urban life.

Employee unions are changing the way local governments are administered. The effects are greater in some cities than in others, and greater in some departments than in others. Nevertheless, change is everywhere, and the rate of change is increasing. Like their counterparts in private industry, public employee unions are demanding and getting an influential—if not equal—voice in determining pay, benefits, and working conditions; and they are being heard increasingly on major personnel policies as well as on minor questions.

Behind this growing strength lies the unions' political power, for at any level of government, politics and administration are hard to separate. To some extent this power is a matter of sheer numbers. There are more than a million union members[1] among some seven million city and county employees, and the number is growing all the time. These numbers mean votes—not only those of the union members, but also of their relatives and friends. The employee vote was significant, for example, in reelecting the mayors of New York in 1961 and of Philadelphia in 1967. Sometimes individual unions endorse candidates formally and take positions on campaign issues. Or they find it advantageous to join together for political action, as in the Committee on Political Education in Philadelphia, the Municipal Improvement League in San Francisco, and the Central Labor Council in New York.

Overt partisan political activity by individual union members is rarely evident. In most of the governments studied here it is restrained by "little Hatch acts"[2] or by local charters or ordinances. These laws vary, but they usually prohibit making appointments on a political basis, or campaigning or soliciting funds for partisan causes by employees. Some of the weaker laws go no further than prohibiting political activity during working hours.

Regardless of the wording of such laws or the zeal with which they are enforced, the political power of the unions is exerted in various informal ways. For as long as labor has been organized, unions have been a convenient point of communication between political leaders and working citizens. Union officials serve on a variety of government advisory committees and meet with chief executives and department heads as lobbyists, claimants, and often as political allies and personal friends. (The business agent of the American Federation of State, County, and Municipal Employees [AFSCME] in Hartford is actually chairman of the labor committee of the Connecticut State Assembly, though this is an unusual example of harmony of interests.)

Public employee unions enjoy not only the power of numbers

1. Estimated by Jack Stieber, Michigan State University, who is conducting a study of union membership as part of the Brookings studies of public employee unionism. See also trend figures in Advisory Commission on Intergovernmental Relations, *Labor-Management Policies for State and Local Government* (1969), pp. 5–12.

2. The federal "Hatch Act" (the basic statute enacted by the Congress in 1939 and subsequent amendments and related laws) prohibits partisan political activity by federal employees, and by state and local employees who are paid from federal funds. The term "little Hatch acts" refers to similar state laws.

and the power of personal acquaintance with officials but also the power that comes from popular support. Citizens, despite their objections to increased taxes, do not ordinarily complain about fair pay rates for public employees—fair, that is, in comparison with private industry—and they usually support referenda authorizing more generous fringe benefits. Above all, citizens hold their governments responsible for the prompt settlement of any labor impasse, actual or threatened, that might shut down a public service.

Public employee strikes, although they are illegal in most states,[3] have clearly increased the power of unions as well as gaining improved pay and benefits for employees. Notable examples include the New York social service caseworkers strike in 1965 over workload; "blue flu" police strikes in Detroit in 1967 and New York in 1968; a San Francisco city hospital strike in 1969 over the handling of grievances; and a social workers' and hospital employees' walkout in 1966 in Los Angeles County to gain formal discussions with management. Garbage strikes in Dade County in 1968, New Orleans in 1968 and 1969, and St. Louis in 1969 were over pay, but they also reflected the aspirations of black citizens for more status and recognition.[4]

However beneficial it is to union members, the total impact of union power may seem appalling to elected officials and to citizens when a city is in the middle of a police slowdown, a prolonged strike by trashmen, or a fiscal crisis to which union demands have contributed. Such events lead understandably to strong statements about the power of unions compared to the powerlessness of government.[5] Yet on the other side are union leaders and members who believe that they are underpaid, subjected to undesirable working conditions, and at the mercy of powerful politicians and bureaucrats. This book provides perspective on these attitudes and relationships by showing how union activities have affected the everyday processes of public administration.

3. Hawaii, Pennsylvania, and Vermont permit public employee strikes, all with some exceptions and limitations.

4. See Bibliography, section 2.

5. See, for example, James Reston in *New York Times,* March 20, 1970; and A. H. Raskin, "The Revolt of the Civil Servants," *Saturday Review,* Vol. 51 (Dec. 7, 1968), p. 89.

What Is Public Administration?

Broadly conceived, public administration is

decision making, planning the work to be done, formulating objectives and goals, working with the legislature and citizen organizations to gain public support and funds for government programs, establishing and revising organization, directing and supervising employees, providing leadership, communicating and receiving communications, determining work methods and procedures, appraising performance, exercising controls, and other functions performed by government executives and supervisors. It is the action part of government, the means by which the purposes and goals of government are realized.[6]

The scope of such a definition invites conflict with definitions of governing, of providing public services. In any government it is difficult to separate ends from means, programs from methods; but the emphasis here is more on the machinery and processes of government than on its program content. This study is concerned with how government gets its work done—how people are hired and directed and how money is budgeted—not with such substantive issues as the size of the housing program, policies on recreation, or the frequency of trash collections.

In order to meet accepted standards of public administration a city or county government will have a personnel system that requires competition for most jobs on the basis of merit, pays employees according to the difficulty and responsibility of their work, provides fringe benefits to enhance employee motivation and security, and operates fair procedures for administering discipline and resolving grievances. Such a government will delegate to its department heads substantial authority over everyday operations, including the assignment of personnel and the use of equipment and supplies. Only unusually expensive or politically sensitive problems will come to the attention of the chief executive or the legislative body. The operating budget, which will be separated from capital expenditures, will be prepared on the basis of a realistic

6. John J. Corson and Joseph P. Harris, *Public Administration in Modern Society* (McGraw-Hill, 1963), p. 12. Many other definitions could have been chosen. For an exhaustive discussion of the nature of public administration, see James C. Charlesworth (ed.), *Theory and Practice of Public Administration: Scope, Objectives, and Methods* (American Academy of Political and Social Science, 1968).

analysis of operating program needs in view of foreseeable revenues from both local and state government sources.

Public administration today does not emphasize pure efficiency to the exclusion of other values, such as high quality service to the clientele, high ethical tone, even-handedness, and rationality. In the pursuit of all its goals the typical city or county government will fall short of managerial perfection because its officials are not necessarily professional managers and because its citizens vary in their ability to obtain protection, service, and advantage from the government. Some of its councilmen will deny nothing to the fire department; others will devise unusual criteria for the location of new health facilities. The chief executive may make special exceptions to the civil service rules. Some employees who should be fired will not be. Work management will be impaired by unforeseen emergencies and the intervention of influential officials in small details. Certain streets may be repaired this year instead of next because of particular citizen pressures; and trash collection service may not be fairly allotted. Financial problems may be aggravated by a reluctance to raise the property tax rate, to introduce a commuter tax, or to increase laboratory fees in the health department. Other problems of administration or finance may be caused or neglected because of restrictive or outmoded state laws.

Such difficulties are inevitable in a responsible democracy. Wallace Sayre points out that

the fundamental problem in a democracy is responsibility to popular control; the responsibility and responsiveness of the administrative agencies and the bureaucracies to the elected officials . . . is of central importance in a government based increasingly on the exercise of discretionary power by the agencies of administration.[7]

The effectiveness of a government in achieving the goals and values of its constituents is the chief measure of the quality of public administration.

The Governments Studied

This report is based on field research undertaken in the first half of 1969 in fifteen cities and four urban counties, which are listed

7. Wallace S. Sayre, "Premises of Public Administration: Past and Emerging," *Public Administration Review*, Vol. 18 (Spring 1958), p. 105.

TABLE I. *Population and Census Region of the Nineteen Local Governments Surveyed, 1960*

Population class, government, and population	Census region
1,000,000 and over	
New York, New York (7,782,000)	Northeast and Mid-Atlantic
Los Angeles County, California (6,039,000)	West
Philadelphia, Pennsylvania (2,003,000)	Northeast and Mid-Atlantic
Detroit, Michigan (1,670,000)	Midwest
500,000–1,000,000	
Dade County, Florida (935,000)	South
St. Louis, Missouri (750,000)[a]	Midwest
Milwaukee, Wisconsin (741,000)	Midwest
San Francisco, California (740,000)[b]	West
Boston, Massachusetts (697,000)	Northeast and Mid-Atlantic
New Orleans, Louisiana (628,000)	South
Buffalo, New York (533,000)	Northeast and Mid-Atlantic
Multnomah County, Oregon (523,000)	West
Cincinnati, Ohio (503,000)	Midwest
250,000–500,000	
New Castle County, Delaware (307,000)	Northeast and Mid-Atlantic
Dayton, Ohio (262,000)	Midwest
100,000–250,000	
Hartford, Connecticut (162,000)	Northeast and Mid-Atlantic
Tacoma, Washington (148,000)	West
75,000–100,000	
Wilmington, Delaware (96,000)	Northeast and Mid-Atlantic
Binghamton, New York (76,000)	Northeast and Mid-Atlantic

Source: U.S. Bureau of the Census, *County and City Data Book, 1967* The numbers in parentheses denote the 1960 population, rounded to the nearest thousand.
   a. City only.
   b. City and county.

by location and population in Table 1. In all of them, political and administrative institutions had felt the impact of union strength.

These nineteen governments in fourteen different states were chosen to reflect wide differences in geographical location, population, form of government, and age and general strength of civil service systems, as well as in the legal framework of employee relations and in the nature and extent of unionization. Where possible, findings from the field research are related to these differences.

On the whole, however, the differences are less important than local history, politics, and personalities in determining how employee groups affect government administration.

Probability sampling was not used in choosing these nineteen localities, and it is not claimed that the findings are representative, in a statistical sense, of administrative practices and union relationships throughout local government in the United States. However, the findings here are reasonably consistent with patterns in other unionized cities and counties, judging by press coverage and by current professional literature.

FORM OF GOVERNMENT

Turning to their characteristics in more detail, nine of the fifteen cities were found to have "strong mayor" governments; four have council-manager governments;[8] and two (in Milwaukee and San Francisco) could be called "less strong mayor" governments.

The nine strong mayor cities are Binghamton, Boston, Buffalo, Detroit, New Orleans, New York, Philadelphia, St. Louis, and Wilmington. This form of government is generally defined as one in which the mayor is elected by the people, not the council; the mayor has the power to appoint and remove department heads, usually without council approval; and there is centralized financial control. The elected council determines general policy but is not responsible for day-to-day administration.[9] The mayor is chief manager and principal policymaker. In five cities (Binghamton, Boston, Detroit, New York, and Wilmington) the mayor can veto any council action, while the mayors of the other four can veto only ordinances.

Several of the cities have delegated some of the executive functions to a chief administrative officer, whose power and authority vary with the locality. The strongest administrative officer is in New Orleans, where he is the mayor's principal assistant and city budget officer and can appoint and remove department heads with the mayor's approval, except where a different appointing author-

8. Called the "commission manager" form in Dayton.

9. Joseph F. Zimmerman, *State and Local Government* (Barnes & Noble, 1962), pp. 152–54; James W. Fesler (ed.), *The 50 States and Their Local Governments* (Alfred A. Knopf, 1967), pp. 473–74.

ity is designated by law. Philadelphia's "managing director" administers ten service departments. The functions of New York's "deputy mayor" (city administrator) depend on who is in the position and on his relationship to the mayor, but this office has generally been concerned with organization and management studies and with the development of new programs. Boston's chief administrative officer is in charge of personnel administration, budget and finance, purchasing, auditing, assessing, data processing, printing, and other supporting administrative services.

In the council-manager cities (Cincinnati, Dayton, Hartford, and Tacoma) the elected council appoints a professional city manager, who serves at the pleasure of that body.[10] The manager has executive authority, including the right to appoint department heads and to prepare the budget. Each of these cities also has a mayor, who presides over the city council and is a ceremonial and political rather than managerial official.

San Francisco, which is both a city and a county, defies classification. The mayor is responsible for general executive leadership and appoints the heads of twenty-four boards, commissions, and agencies. A chief administrative officer, appointed by the mayor, oversees nine departments, including finances and records, public health, public works, purchasing, and real estate. The board of supervisors, elected at large, plays a strong part in both policy and administration. In Milwaukee there are also many boards and commissions, some of which appoint department heads. This weakens the mayor's authority, but he does have the power to veto actions of the common council, subject to having the veto overridden by a two-thirds vote.

Each of the four counties has a different governmental system. The elected Dade County "commission" appoints a professional manager, who has broad executive powers. Similarly, in Los Angeles County the board of supervisors appoints a chief administrative officer. While he cannot select department heads, he does run the budget and the county's administrative functions. In Multnomah County, executive authority is vested in the chairman of the board of commissioners. He can establish jobs, allocate funds, and, with

10. At the time of the field research there was a bitter feud between the mayor and the city manager of Tacoma. An anti-manager council majority was later elected, and the manager resigned. Since then the position has been filled, but its functions have been less completely and aggressively exercised.

the approval of the other commissioners, appoint and remove department heads. New Castle County has a part-time elected council and a full-time county executive, elected for a four-year term. This official, like a strong mayor, appoints and removes department heads (instances in which council approval is necessary are specified in the charter), proposes a budget, and exercises some veto powers. According to the charter, he may appoint a chief administrative officer to share his responsibilities, and has done so.

MERIT SYSTEMS

In all but a few of these nineteen governments, civil service merit systems have traditionally received substantial support. Several (New York, Detroit, Cincinnati) date back to the early years of this century. The newer merit systems are found in New Castle County, where the civil service system was introduced in 1967, and in Dade County, where it was adopted in 1957.[11]

In a strong merit system a large majority of the jobs are covered by rules requiring competition on the basis of demonstrated merit for appointment or promotion and giving employees who have tenure protection against arbitrary dismissal or other penalties.[12] A strong merit system also has a technically qualified staff performing a wide range of personnel functions. Judged by these criteria, the weaker systems in the governments studied are in Binghamton, where the local civil service commission forwards examining and classification work to the state government and where many positions are exempted from the competitive service; and in Boston, where civil service examining functions belong to the state government but have little impact on widespread patronage practices in the city government, and where the city has only a small personnel division, whose staff is engaged in relatively routine work. Among the others quality varies. There have never been any studies that ranked civil service systems in local governments. Among profes-

11. Merit systems in local governments were made possible by the Florida legislature in 1955. The Dade County metropolitan government charter in 1957 authorized a change to a merit system by commission action.

12. For an authoritative discussion of merit principles and merit system standards, see *Progress in Intergovernmental Personnel Relations*, Report of the Advisory Committee on Merit System Standards, joint publication of U.S. Department of Health, Education, and Welfare, U.S. Department of Defense, and U.S. Department of Labor (Government Printing Office, 1969), especially pp. 14–16.

sional personnel managers, however, Detroit, Los Angeles County, Milwaukee, and New Orleans have enjoyed good reputations, based on relatively strong staffing, community and political acceptance of merit principles, and rigorous competitive requirements for filling positions.

The cities and counties are not entirely free to set their own terms and conditions of employment. All are subject to federal merit system standards for employees who administer certain programs financed from federal grants—mainly health, welfare, and employment service programs.[13] Besides, eleven of the fourteen states in which the research was done have state requirements as to qualifications, pay, hours, fringe benefits, and working conditions in their local governments. Such state "mandating," as well as the federal requirements, have been discussed extensively in the 1969 report on labor-management policies by the Advisory Commission on Intergovernmental Relations.[14] The report concludes that sound labor-management programs in local governments will be benefited if state requirements are kept to a minimum and federal requirements are not extended.[15] The present book reflects the impact of union activity within the framework of *all* requirements and limitations—local, state, federal. The impact has been greatest in areas where the local governments are most free to make their own decisions.

Administration of these local governments is influenced by many other factors, such as relationships with their state governments, their fiscal situations, the existence of separately managed and financed public agencies, ethnic and other sociological pressures, and general management attitudes and competence. These are difficult to summarize a priori; therefore, they will be brought in as appropriate in later chapters.

State Laws on Collective Bargaining

Another factor affecting, and in part controlling, the role played by unions is the content of state laws covering organization and

13. For the coverage and content of these standards, see *ibid.*, pp. 93–100.
14. *Labor-Management Policies,* pp. 46–47, 83–89, 260–63.
15. *Ibid.,* pp. 110–13.

collective bargaining for public employees.[16] Such laws range from none at all in Louisiana to an explicit directive to public employers in nine of the fourteen states studied to bargain with their employees. Collective bargaining is mandatory in Connecticut, Delaware (for cities that elect coverage), Massachusetts, Michigan, New York, Oregon, Pennsylvania, Washington, and Wisconsin. The laws in Connecticut, Delaware, Massachusetts, and Washington prohibit bargaining on certain specified aspects of the merit systems. Public employees in Florida are allowed to bargain collectively under a court interpretation of the 1968 state constitution.[17] Even before that decision the manager of Dade County had decided that the county would negotiate "memoranda of understanding" (in effect, agreements) with employee groups.

In California and Missouri, public employers are required to meet and confer with employee organizations. Although the Missouri constitution forbids localities to negotiate contracts with unions, under a 1967 statute, union and local government officials may discuss issues and present their written recommendations "to the appropriate administrative, legislative or other governing body in the form of an ordinance, resolution, bill or other form required for adoption, modification or rejection."[18] In August 1969 the first informal agreement written under this law for public employees in the St. Louis area was negotiated between sewage workers and the Metropolitan Sewer District, an independent unit.

Interpretations of the California law, which became effective January 1, 1969, are just beginning to be made, and there are problems to be resolved. For example, the law points to the mutual *obligation* of both parties to try to reach agreement, yet a *nonbinding* memorandum of understanding is presented to the local governing body, which is the sole determining authority for approval and implementation. Localities are applying the law at different rates of speed. Los Angeles County has passed a detailed or-

16. There are, of course, other types of legal guidelines on public employee labor relations: court rulings, opinions of attorneys general, executive orders, and others. This discussion of state laws is merely illustrative. See Harry H. Wellington and Ralph K. Winter, Jr., *The Unions and the Cities* (Brookings Institution, 1971), particularly Chap. 2.

17. *Dade County Classroom Teachers Association, Inc. v. Ryan*, Fla., 225 So. 2d 903 (Supreme Court of Florida, July 9, 1969).

18. State of Missouri, House Bill 106, 74 General Assembly, 1967, sec. 105.520.

dinance, has established an employee relations commission for determining representation units and other conditions of relationships, and has concluded many "memoranda of understanding" (that is, agreements) with employee groups. In San Francisco the local civil service commission appointed a management team headed by the city's chief administrative officer to negotiate an employee relations ordinance with an employee organization team.

State laws in Ohio do not require the employer to confer with unions. Instead, employee organizations have the right to express or communicate "a view, grievance, complaint or opinion on any matter related to the conditions or compensation of public employment. . . ."[19] But the lack of statutory language has not prevented Ohio localities from negotiating with employee organizations. Both the Cincinnati Council and the Dayton Commission have adopted resolutions governing these cities' dealings with employee groups and permitting written union contracts.

Where a state law governs the relationships between unions and urban governments, there must be a supervisory agency to administer the statute. The agency may, for example, determine the appropriateness of bargaining units, interpret conditions for recognition of a union, act on charges of unfair labor practices, and help resolve impasses. In New York State and Oregon such functions are assigned to special public employee relations boards. In eight of the other states studied here this work is done by the same state agency that is responsible for private labor relations—Connecticut, Delaware, Massachusetts, Michigan, Missouri, Pennsylvania, Washington, and Wisconsin. There are no such boards in California and Ohio.

There are further complications. New York State (which has its own public relations board) and California (which does not) both permit these regulatory and service functions to be exercised locally. Among the cities studied, New York City has its own office of collective bargaining under a tripartite (public-management-union) board to supervise labor relations in the city service and provide aid in resolution of impasses. Buffalo has its own public employee relations board for the same purposes. California law permits localities to issue their own rules on employee relations.

19. Sec. 4117.01 of the Ohio Revised Code.

Los Angeles had already set up its employee relations commission at the time of the field research, and San Francisco has been discussing the establishment of a similar organization with the unions concerned. Ohio localities, as has already been noted, received no guidance or service under state law and manage their union relationships under existing ordinances or agreements.

The Unions in the Cities and Counties

Each of the nineteen local governments deals with a different combination of unions, some with scores, others with only a few.[20] The unions can be classified under four main types according to their composition and affiliations:

1. *Affiliated unions that are found also in the private sector.* The Teamsters union, for example, is strong in Detroit and represents nearly all levels of employees in the gigantic New York City Housing Authority. Locals of the Service Employees International Union (SEIU) are numerous and influential in Los Angeles County and San Francisco. Blue-collar employees in the recognized trades and crafts are represented in some cities by locals of their own trade or craft unions, with membership in both the public and the private spheres. In others they are represented by the AFSCME, the SEIU, or some local association.

2. *Strong unions with members only in governments.* In particular, locals of AFSCME are present in all of the nineteen governments studied. They tend to be stronger in the East and Midwest than in the West and South, although there is rapid growth in the latter region. The International Association of Fire Fighters (IAFF) represents firemen in all of these cities and counties that have fire departments. As for police, lodges of the Fraternal Order of Police, a loose confederation, are established in five of the locali-

20. See Jack Stieber, "Employee Representation in Municipal Government," *The Municipal Year Book, 1969* (Washington, D.C.: International City Management Association, 1969), pp. 31–57. See also Winston W. Crouch, "The American City and Its Organized Employees," *Urban Data Service*, Vol. 1 (March 1969 issue). This is also the subject of a study being prepared by Jack Stieber for the Brookings Institution.

ties studied. Otherwise, police are represented by a variety of independent and affiliated organizations.

3. *Professional associations.* These are receiving recognition, bargaining collectively, and exerting pressure in other ways both nationally and locally. Nursing associations and societies of professional engineers are examples.

4. *Local civil service associations.* These too may function like unions, notably in Los Angeles County and San Francisco.[21]

Union security[22] provisions revealed several patterns. All of the governments recognize and deal with unions, formally or informally. All permit dues checkoffs, a matter of great importance to the maintenance of a union. All of the cities and counties, except Los Angeles County and St. Louis, had one or more formal agreements with unions at the time of the field research.[23] Four governments (Hartford, New Castle County, Philadelphia, and Wilmington) have signed union shop agreements; that is, agreements specifying that persons employed in specified classes of jobs must join the union. Boston has an agency shop arrangement—employees who are in a bargaining unit but are not union members must pay fees that compensate the unions for their services that benefit all employees.[24]

Method of Study and Presentation

The findings and conclusions in this book are based primarily on interviews in the nineteen local governments and on analyses of such documents as charters, laws, civil service rules, pay schedules, union agreements, newspaper stories, and many others. Interviewing began late in 1968 after a period devoted to a study of the liter-

21. The Civil Service Association in San Francisco recently affiliated with the Marine Engineers Beneficial Association. See Bureau of National Affairs, *Government Employee Relations Report*, No. 388 (Feb. 15, 1971), p. B-19.

22. Union security refers to the protection of union status by provisions in an agreement establishing a closed union, or agency shop, or maintenance-of-membership.

23. The only agreement in New Orleans was with a relatively independent agency, the sewerage and water board.

24. Dayton and Detroit had agency shop agreements at the time of the field research. These have since been rendered ineffective by court decisions.

ature, selection of the governments, consultation with other Brookings researchers, and preparation of the interview questionnaires. Field research was concluded in the summer of 1969.

Each city or county was visited for a period of from one to two weeks by an experienced interviewer, who questioned such persons as the chief executive (if he was available for interview), the personnel or civil service director, the labor relations specialist (if any), the budget and finance officer, the heads of several strongly unionized departments, several union leaders, and one or two "government observers," that is, representatives of taxpayer alliances, of the League of Women Voters, or other such groups. Interviewers used five standard interview schedules, containing open-ended questions. Not all activities were included. Education was not covered at all, and only a few publicly owned utilities (bus lines, electric plants, water or sanitation systems) were included.

The following chapters present the major patterns of change in public administration resulting from union activities in these governments, with examples drawn from the various cities and counties. The facts presented, unless otherwise indicated, are drawn from interviews and related administrative documents in the nineteen governments. Little of the information is quantified except that relating to pay, fringe benefits, and finances, and no sophisticated statistical analyses have been included.

The term "management" here refers to the city or county government officials (both legislative and executive) with whom union representatives deal. The context will usually make clear whether "management" refers to the chief executive, the government bargainers, a department head, or some combination of public officials.

Finally, despite certain unavoidable overlaps, this book does not deal authoritatively with the central topics of other studies in this Brookings series, which consider legal issues in public employee unionism, the nature of unionism in the public sector, the structure of collective bargaining, and the economic effects of unionism on wages in the public sector.

CHAPTER TWO

The Employment Relationship

Relationships between governments and their employees have been changing for years in both concept and tone. The activities of unions have accelerated and emphasized these changes, bringing new policies and, in some governments, altered organizational structures. This chapter summarizes the changes, and later chapters will present the details of the impact of unionism on employment, pay, on-the-job management, and finance.

Nineteenth century fiction and twentieth century comic strips have helped foster the idea that the employment relationship in the United States is authoritarian: A private employer offers a job. A job seeker—presumably grateful for the opportunity—accepts the position and subjects himself to such discipline and conditions as the employer may offer. This concept becomes shaky at once because the job seeker does not have to take that particular job; he may bargain for a different one. Nor does he have to stay in the job if he does not like it. He may leave and find another one, especially if his skills are in short supply. He may also limit the enthusiasm he puts into his work. "People can be managed and directed only with their consent. . . . There is no legal compulsion upon the workers to cooperate."[1]

1. Neil W. Chamberlain and James W. Kuhn, *Collective Bargaining* (2nd ed., McGraw-Hill, 1965), pp. 89–90.

Employment, then, is a bargain, a transaction. Starting with the right to operate the enterprise, management makes agreements concerning hours, pay, benefits, and working conditions with employees or groups of employees to obtain and keep their services. Management retains the right to make business decisions that do not directly affect employees, and these are often specified in union contracts.[2] If the bargain becomes unacceptable to one party or the other, an individual employee may quit or be fired; a group of employees may strike or be locked out.

The Employment Bargain in Government

The employment relationship in government, like that in the private sector, appears more authoritarian at first than it really is. Government's apparently unlimited authority over its employees was originally based on its *sovereignty*. The idea that government employees have only the rights that the government permits them is related to the concepts that the king can do no wrong and that government can be sued only with its consent. The sovereignty doctrine has often been used to defend infringements of civil liberties in federal loyalty-security programs and to uphold a denial of the right of employee organizations to negotiate the terms of employment.

However, the doctrine of sovereignty as applied to employment has been substantially dismembered by legal and academic critics,[3] joined by government lawmakers and rulemakers. Governments, however supreme, make deals. They also give citizens, including citizens who are employees, orderly means of presenting and discussing their needs. Besides, the sovereignty doctrine is questionable in local governments, which have only as much authority as their states give them. So the times are catching up with sover-

2. See discussions of management security and prerogatives in labor relations texts, for example, Chamberlain and Kuhn, *Collective Bargaining*, pp. 89–99; Alfred Kuhn, *Labor: Institutions and Economics* (rev. ed., Harcourt, Brace and World, 1967), pp. 57–62.

3. For treatments of the sovereignty doctrine and its relevance to the ability of public employees to organize, bargain, and strike see section 1 of the Bibliography, especially the works by Hanslowe, Godine, and Wellington and Winter ("The Limits of Collective Bargaining in Public Employment").

eignty as a deterrent to unionism, and collective bargaining is now permitted in differing degree by a great variety of laws, executive orders, and court decisions.[4]

A more relevant and current objection to collective bargaining in the public service is based on the doctrine of the illegal delegation of power. This principle, which forbids a government to share its powers with others, sets some limits on the scope of negotiations,[5] but has not been a significant obstacle to the development of bargaining.

The most important asset that employees can use in bargaining is the assurance of their presence on the job. This makes the theoretical problem more complex and more relevant to the general welfare. There is controversy among experts as to whether the right to bargain implies the right to strike[6] and whether public employees have the right to strike at all. These issues are beyond the scope of this book, but it should be noted that the doctrine of sovereignty is now joined by that of the *essentiality* of government services. Thus, those who deny the right of public employees to strike (including the Congress and nearly all state legislatures) do so both as a matter of concept (people cannot strike against *the people*) and as a matter of public duty (public services must not stop).[7] Public employees nevertheless have struck—repeatedly, often advantageously, and usually with impunity. Whether they strike too much (assuming that they should strike at all) is another issue that will not be resolved here. One expert's findings are pertinent, however. His figures show that more than 15,700 agreements in the public sector were negotiated in five selected states in recent years and that 203 strikes occurred.[8] Even a relatively small

4. See section 3 of the Bibliography.

5. Harry H. Wellington and Ralph K. Winter, "The Limits of Collective Bargaining in Public Employment," *Yale Law Journal,* Vol. 78 (June 1969), pp. 1109–11, 1125–26.

6. See sections 1 and 2 of the Bibliography.

7. The essentiality question is discussed in Leonard D. White, "Strikes in the Public Service," *Public Personnel Review,* Vol. 10 (January 1949), pp. 3–10; in John F. Burton, Jr., and Charles Krider, "The Role and Consequences of Strikes by Public Employees," *Yale Law Journal,* Vol. 79 (January 1970), pp. 418–40; and in Harry H. Wellington and Ralph K. Winter, *The Unions and the Cities* (Brookings Institution, 1971), Chaps. 1, 11, and 12.

8. Robert L. Stutz, "The Resolution of Impasses in the Public Sector," *The Urban Lawyer,* Vol. 1 (Fall 1969), p. 321. (The states are Wisconsin, Michigan, New York, Massachusetts, and Connecticut.)

number can have impressive effects, of course, and later chapters in this study refer to some stoppages that had an impact on administration as well as on services rendered. The threat, or even the possibility, of a strike can also have a major impact upon the functioning of a local government.

A government's bargain with its employees is similar in several respects to that of the private employer. Both must shop in the employment market and must pay enough in money and otherwise to attract and retain qualified workers. Both must get their employees to agree to certain conditions and limitations—to accept unusual working hours, to perform hazardous or disagreeable duties, to keep the employer's secrets. Both must somehow meet the individual's basic needs for recognition, security, progress, and sense of belonging.

There are other similarities that are more important than the apparent or legalistic differences. Many government employees, for example, are covered by civil service merit systems, and any well managed business also requires its applicants to demonstrate their fitness for their jobs. On the other hand, if nepotism and patronage appear in some governments, they show up in the commercial world also. Government employees are protected by civil service and other laws from arbitrary discipline or removal, and comparable protection (in company policies and labor contracts) is found in business.

The most significant difference, for purposes of this discussion, is that labor relations has an economic foundation in industry but a political base in government. The private employer must stay in business and sell his goods and his services in order to pay his employees. Unions normally do not make such high demands that they drive the employer out of business or into a drastic curtailment of his operations. If a strike occurs, it is a test of economic strength or staying power and is perfectly legal. Governments, on the other hand, have to stay in business, and their payrolls are met from taxes or fees imposed on the public. Their unions do not hesitate to press for higher pay and other benefits that will be paid for by the taxpayer. If a strike occurs, it becomes a complex political problem involving indignation over an illegal stoppage, pressure on public officials to settle so that services may be restored, sympathy for the needs of public employees, problems of financing the settlement, and other elements too.

Even these differences are not clear-cut. Many a strike in private industry involves the public interest immediately and strongly, thus inviting government intervention and becoming a political problem. Strikes in communication, transportation, and food industries are examples. The "economic test of strength," moreover, does not threaten the private employer if he can pass on the cost of the settlement to his customers. Another difference becomes a similarity when illegal strikes in the public service, although neither encouraged nor condoned, are clearly accepted by public officials as problems to be solved by negotiation.

In both public and private sectors, organized employees use power to affect the distribution of resources and the management of men and materials. In the private sector they do this primarily *as employees*. In the public sector they exert influence *as employees, as pressure groups, and as voting citizens*. "Management" officials in government, who are responsible directly or indirectly to the voters, are in this sense in a weaker position than are corporation managers in dealing with the demands of the organized employees. This three-dimensioned structure of public employee power greatly complicates the employment transaction in government and elevates it to a major problem in public administration, public law, and public finance.

Where Does Management Start?

One more difference (which is also a similarity) between public and private labor relations deserves separate attention and concerns the definition of "management." This term has to be used more loosely in the public sector. Here "management" means the decision-making authorities of government, both legislative and executive, who can grant or deny what the unions want. This covers a wide range of authority: the legislative body enacting a new pension plan, a park superintendent approving a change in work shifts, or a foreman settling a minor grievance.

In any work force it is hard to draw the line between "management" and "employees." A branch chief is an employee for some purposes; he is management for others. In the private sector, foremen are clearly part of management, but they have their problems as employees and rarely have their own bargaining units. The distinction is especially difficult in government because management authority is so diffused. (This in itself is a problem to union leaders who can speak for their organizations but cannot find city officials who are authorized or willing to give final answers.) Varying amounts of authority are given to executives by city or county charters, and lesser amounts are redelegated to those at lower levels. Suppose, for example, that a hospital orderly is to be discharged for insubordinate behavior. Who is "management": the nurse who complains, the personnel officer who draws up the papers, the service chief who signs them, the superintendent who has the authority to discharge, or the director of the department of hospitals? Answer: all of them, as far as the employee and his union are concerned.

The line between employees and management is most feasibly drawn (as it is in private industry) at the point where the work of genuine supervision begins: issuing orders, approving time off, giving on-the-job instruction, reviewing work, and recommending disciplinary action. There are exceptions and problems because of the way the particular department and union are organized. Some unions (social workers' and fire fighters' unions, for example) represent several levels within the same department. In general the labor relations situation is complicated adversely if a supervisor and his subordinates belong to the same bargaining unit. Such complications are lessened or avoided if the supervisor behaves as a supervisor—as "management"—and regards his union membership only as a means of having salaries and benefits negotiated for him. This has been traditional with fire department officers, nearly all of whom were union members in the cities that were studied.

Decisions on where to draw the line should be made at the time the makeup of the bargaining unit is decided upon. Discussions of this matter are easier if the government has available a clear organizational chart showing the positions and employees concerned. Milwaukee maintains such a "visual organizational inventory," which serves a wide variety of administrative purposes.[9]

Management Rights

"Management's survival in collective bargaining," says Alfred Kuhn, "refers to its ability to remain master in its own house and

9. Arnold E. Logan and Robert C. Garnier, "Milwaukee's Visual Organizational Inventory," *Public Personnel Review*, Vol. 28 (July 1967), pp. 169–73.

to retain managerial authority, without which it ceases to be management."[10] The survival of management in this sense is assisted in part by management rights clauses in laws, ordinances, or union contracts. Such clauses, which are commonplace in private industry, were found in only about half of the cities and counties in this study.[11] Among these governments, and even among unions within a government, such clauses vary in scope and explicitness. Typically they recite management's right to hire, direct, discipline, and fire employees and to decide how programs shall be administered. Unions acknowledge these rights in return for being recognized and for being given the right to bargain on specified matters and to submit grievances. Essentially they do not challenge or covet management's right to manage but insist on opportunities to negotiate and be heard on the *effect* of management's decisions on pay, hours, and working conditions.

This distinction is well illustrated in the basic documents governing employee relations in Los Angeles County and New York City. The Los Angeles ordinance says:

The exercise of such [county] rights does not preclude employees or their representatives from conferring or raising grievances about the practical consequences that decisions on these matters may have on wages, hours, and other terms and conditions of employment.[12]

The New York City executive order gives unions a voice on matters usually reserved to management. After stating the city's right, among others, to

determine the standards of services to be offered by its agencies; . . . determine the methods, means and personnel by which government operations are to be conducted; . . . exercise complete control and discretion over its organization and the technology of performing its work,

the order continues:

The City's decisions on those matters are not within the scope of collective bargaining, but, notwithstanding the above, questions concerning the practical impact that decisions on the above matters have on

10. Kuhn, *Labor: Institutions and Economics*, p. 83.

11. None were found in Binghamton, Buffalo, Multnomah County, New Orleans, Philadelphia, San Francisco, Tacoma, and Wilmington. Dade County had none in its first contracts but added them the following year. St. Louis and Los Angeles County had no agreements at the time of the field research.

12. *Employee Relations Ordinance of the County of Los Angeles*, Ordinance No. 9646 (October 1968), p. 3.

employees, *such as questions of workload or manning,* are within the scope of collective bargaining.[13]

Both documents, in effect, invite unions to make their voices heard concerning decisions reserved to management. All they have to do is show "practical consequences" or "practical impact" on employees. In the latter instance a decision of the New York City Board of Collective Bargaining provides for rapid consideration by that board of cases where the city does not relieve such an "'impact.'"[14]

EXAMPLES OF CLAUSES

All management rights clauses that were reviewed in this study say essentially that "management has the right to run the government (or department), subject to the provisions of this agreement." Some are stated very generally, though strongly, such as that part of the contract with the Social Service Employees Union (SSEU) in New York:

> It is recognized that the Department of Social Services has complete authority over the policies and the administration of the Department and of the Social Service program exercisable under the provisions of law and in fulfillment of its rights and responsibilities under the Contract.[15]

However, the phrase "complete authority" becomes less impressive when read with the wealth of detailed provisions on hours, workload, and working conditions in other sections of the contract (see Chapter 5).

Further examples of brief, generally phrased management rights clauses are Dayton's agreement with the Dayton Public Service Union, Cincinnati's with Council 51 of the American Federation of State, County, and Municipal Employees (AFSCME), and Tacoma's with its fire fighters' union. Other agreements specify management rights in more detail, as well as making overall statements

---

13. New York City, Executive Order No. 52, "The Conduct of Labor Relations Between the City of New York and Its Employees" (Sept. 29, 1967), sec. 5C (italics supplied).

14. New York City, Board of Collective Bargaining, Decision No. B-9-68, Nov. 12, 1968.

15. Contract between the City of New York and the Department of Social Services and the Social Service Employees Union, Sept. 21, 1967, Article XVII, p. 32.

about personnel administration and work management. Hartford's and New Castle County's are examples.

Despite the centralization of management's bargaining responsibilities, discussed below, management may agree to have its prerogatives stated differently in different contracts—if they are mentioned at all. In New York, for example, there are brief, general management rights clauses in the SSEU and AFSCME Local 1549 agreements but none in those with AFSCME District Council 37, or with the police, fire, and sanitation unions. Detroit's contracts vary widely as to whether equal employment opportunity provisions and statements concerning the city's right to contract out its work are included. The many Milwaukee agreements vary too, particularly as to whether they deal with contracting-out and with departmental reorganizations.

AN UNCERTAIN BOUNDARY

This discussion of relationships and clauses shows that management rights are anything but clear-cut. In many a case a union cannot control or bargain over a major decision on funding, manpower, or operations, but *can* negotiate or file grievances over the details of its implementation. The boundary is uncertain, the distinction fuzzy, because management really directs the work *with the consent of employees.* This is well recognized in the private sector by scholars and observers.[16] The problem is even more difficult, the distinction less clear, in the public sector because of the essentially political nature of the relationship. Thus, management and unions have different areas of primary concern, and different types of initiatives, and these areas and initiatives inevitably overlap.

Management rights clauses originally were intended to keep unions out of specified management decisions entirely, and unions do indeed stay out of these areas in large part, as Chapter 5 shows. As unions gain strength, however, such clauses serve less as fences and more as signposts, showing the activities where management

16. See Charles C. Killingsworth, "The Presidential Address: Management Rights Revisited," *Arbitration and Social Change: Proceedings of the 22nd Annual Meeting, National Academy of Arbitrators* (Bureau of National Affairs, 1970), pp. 1–20. See also note 2 above.

will take the initiative, subject possibly to union consultation, objection, and appeal. In formal agreements, unions recognize areas of primary concern to management in return for the right to bargain on many other conditions of employment. Hence management rights clauses are one more important part of the never-ending, always changing transaction between employees and management.

Organization for Labor Relations

Moving now from legalisms to institutions in the employment relationship, we take a look at the impact of growing unionism on the personnel management organization of the cities and counties.

To begin with, the legislative bodies have had to devote more time and more political emphasis to personnel matters, particularly where they have trouble financing the pay increases and other changes that have been negotiated. They have the difficult problem of helping the unions—an important group of voters—without looking like pushovers to the taxpayers.

The chief executive, whether he is a mayor or city manager, has both a political and an administrative role to play in labor relations. Politically he shares responsibility with the legislative body for the impact of settlements. Administratively he acts as supervisor and adviser of the management negotiators, or he may be a negotiator himself.

Several different organizational patterns of labor negotiating responsibilities were found among the governments studied—patterns that have changed in several cases (see Table 2).

There are advantages if the chief negotiator is also chief executive: questions can be answered quickly and authoritatively, thus saving time and avoiding lower-level maneuvering; the manager or chairman can commit the government to decisions, subject to review only by the legislative body of matters within its authority. Yet prevailing management opinion opposes such an arrangement. Officials of most of these governments believe that the chief executive should stay "above the battle," contributing his judgment as needed on fiscal and personnel problems and presenting the results of bargaining to the city council. They also emphasize that it is

TABLE 2. *Official with Primary Bargaining Responsibility in the Nineteen Local Governments Surveyed, 1969*

Government	Official with primary responsibility
Governments with collective bargaining agreements	
Dade County	Chief executive (later changed to a staff assistant)
Multnomah County	Chief executive
Tacoma	Chief executive
Boston	Labor relations specialist (heavy responsibility carried by a staff attorney)
Detroit	Labor relations specialist
Milwaukee	Labor relations specialist (responsibility formerly exercised by personnel director)
New York	Labor relations specialist
Cincinnati	Civil service or personnel director
Dayton	Civil service or personnel director
Hartford	Civil service or personnel director
New Castle County	Civil service or personnel director (initial agreements under collective bargaining negotiated by a consultant)
Philadelphia	Civil service or personnel director (long-term labor relations consultants retained before establishment of an office of labor relations)
Wilmington	Civil service or personnel director (jointly with city solicitor)
Binghamton	Executive assistant to mayor (later changed to corporation counsel)
Buffalo	Budget director (later changed to personnel director)
Governments without collective bargaining agreements	
Los Angeles County	Personnel director (later made responsible for "meet and confer" sessions)
New Orleans	None
St. Louis	Personnel director (responsible for "meet and confer" sessions tantamount to bargaining)
San Francisco	None

Source: Survey by authors.

unnecessary for the chief executive to be involved in all the time-consuming details of bargaining.

When the chief executive assigns bargaining responsibility, he usually gives it either to a labor relations unit or to the personnel or civil service office. In either case the responsibility is likely to be shared by other members of a bargaining team, usually including representatives of the budget and legal staffs and of one or more operating divisions. Budget directors are members of management bargaining teams in Binghamton, Dayton, Hartford, Multnomah County, and Philadelphia, and are never far removed from the negotiators elsewhere.

The four cities that rely on labor relations staffs or specialists are all large and have many recognized bargaining units: 26 in Boston, 18 in Milwaukee, 120 in Detroit, and about 200 in New York. The latter two have established offices that are responsible for bargaining and other dealings with unions. In 1965 Detroit's bureau of labor relations took over from the city's budget bureau the salary and wage setting function and the staff responsible for it. The civil service commission staff retains responsibility for job classification work as well as the remaining personnel functions. The commission found it necessary to set up a new "hearing section," consisting of three professionals who take part in negotiations and in work on grievances.

Bargaining responsibilities in New York City, formerly exercised jointly by the budget director and personnel director, have been assigned to an office of labor relations.[17] Coordination is maintained through a labor policy committee chaired by the deputy mayor (city administrator) and made up of the other deputy mayor, the director of the bureau of the budget, the director of the department of personnel, the corporation counsel, and the director of the office of labor relations.

PRESENT AND FUTURE ORGANIZATION

One cannot generalize with confidence from these facts, but a few conclusions stand out. The largest group of cities and counties are relying on their personnel or civil service staffs to assume labor relations responsibilities. Only large cities with a multiplicity of bargaining units have set up full-time labor specialists or units. More cities can be expected to follow their lead as unions become more aggressive and numerous in the future and as the scope of bargaining increases. At the same time their personnel offices will be un-

17. Not to be confused with the office of collective bargaining (see p. 12), which regulates and supervises the city's labor relations processes.

der increasing pressure, as a result of union activities, to furnish back-up information for negotiations, to cope with requests for changes in the job classification plan, to assist with grievance proceedings, to administer complex fringe benefits, to interpret promotion rules, and to deal with many other problems. Coordination between personnel and labor relations staffs will obviously be essential. The larger, more thoroughly unionized governments can be expected to move toward the industrial pattern—a department of labor relations headed by a vice mayor or an assistant manager for labor relations, who will supervise not only bargaining and employee relations but also selection and training activities.

ROLE OF DEPARTMENT HEADS

Department heads in urban governments, like those in large industries, are in an awkward position in relation to collective bargaining. For many purposes they *are* management, for example, in planning work operations, enforcing discipline, or settling grievances. Yet it is obviously impractical for heads of all departments to participate in collective bargaining, even though the results are very important to their work. Sixteen department heads in a city may be strongly affected by a bargained provision concerning overtime, but all cannot discuss it simultaneously with a union. This study found that department heads in the governments that use collective bargaining generally make recommendations and give information to the management bargaining team. As bargaining proceeds, there are often occasions when the bargainers ask department heads to provide data or to comment on provisions that are being considered. Failure to consult them can result in the kind of problem faced by the police chief of one city:

The rules prior to 1969 provided for equal time off if the policeman worked a holiday. [The police union] asked for greater compensation, and the city negotiators agreed to give a day off even if the holiday fell on the officer's off day, and two off if he actually worked the holiday. The chief did not know it until he saw the approved contract—too late to change. He states he will lose the equivalent of eleven men through this change, yet he feels it was something the [police union] threw in for bargaining purposes. Good lesson for those who ignore line management.[18]

18. This quotation is from interview notes.

The difficulty is not that the change lacked merit but that the chief was not consulted or given a chance to plan for the necessary adjustments in manning and budgeting.

Department heads in a few of the cities (Milwaukee, New York, Tacoma, Wilmington) attend bargaining sessions as advisers. In still others, such as Hartford, a few department heads serve on the city bargaining team. In Detroit and New York, economic issues are negotiated centrally, but department heads participate in the bargaining on other terms and conditions of employment, with the results embodied in supplemental agreements.

Management's working level relationships with unions are normally maintained by department heads and lower-level supervisors on an informal basis. In addition three of the governments provide for union-management counsils to discuss work problems of concern to the unions. In Dade County such councils are required by the negotiated memoranda of understanding between the county and the unions. In Dayton joint committees have been established in the fire and police departments "to discuss subjects of mutual concern." New York City is the third urban government that uses councils; there are organized systems of consultation in eight out of the eighteen departments where interviews were conducted for this study, although some were quite informal.

TRAINING SUPERVISORS IN LABOR RELATIONS

The key position of foreman or first-line supervisor in labor relations is recognized everywhere in policies and in the literature on personnel management, and cities and counties in this study are no exception. The supervisor confronts union members and stewards at the point where the work is really done, where assignments are made and reviewed, where on-the-job training is given, and where promotions may be recommended, discipline enforced, and grievances begun. It is obvious that almost any amount of supervisory training in labor relations matters will be beneficial. Yet most of the urban governments studied here offer no organized training of this sort.

There are a few exceptions. Los Angeles County has held an all-day seminar for supervisors, often sends selected officials to special institutes, and plans to expand its efforts along these lines. With the help of the University of Delaware, Wilmington has presented a foremen's training program of eight two-hour sessions. The New York City department of personnel has given courses for supervisors both with its own training staff and under contract with the Cornell School of Industrial and Labor Relations. The department is now preparing representatives of operating departments to train supervisors. The Dade County personnel office has given a standard, comprehensive "orientation" course for supervisors, including pointers on all aspects of personnel administration, and has circulated copies of helpful literature on labor relations in the public service, much of it published by the Public Personnel Association. Since the field research for this study was completed, Hartford has started a course for first-line supervisors and has prepared a program for training intermediate supervisors and department heads.

The most ambitious programs encountered were in Detroit and Milwaukee. Both cities have trained hundreds of supervisors in a variety of short courses given by the city civil service commission, local universities, and others. (See Appendix A for more detail.) Elsewhere cities were not formally training supervisors in labor relations. Interviewees generally acknowledged the need for such training and sometimes deplored their inability to meet it, pleading the necessity of using money and staff on higher-priority activities. (One is reminded of the fable about the woodsman who was too busy cutting a tree to sharpen his axe.)

The deficiency may have been remedied somewhat in the period since the field research was undertaken. The conduct of institutes, seminars, and workshops on public employee labor relations has become an active business for both nonprofit and profit-making enterprises.

The Tone of the Relationship

Even where unionism has caused no organizational change, there has been a shift in the tone or atmosphere of the employment relationship. This new relationship reflects a transaction between relatively equal parties, each with strengths, each with limitations resulting from the other's strengths. If the present and foreseeable future situation is compared with the nonunion or weak-union past, employees appear to be less acceptant and more challenging; and management is less dominant, more wary, more subject to questioning and resistance by employees, and therefore more responsible. Thus there has been a weakening of what might be called "management-by-itself." The era of unilateralism, of unquestioned sovereignty, is about over, and the age of bilateralism—consultation, negotiation, and bargaining—is already here. An adversary confrontation is replacing a paternalistic or master-servant relationship.

Inevitably, tensions in the employment situation emerge. The basic strain between management and employees is stronger, but it is out in the open and more clearly understood than were the diffused tensions of the days when employees were unrepresented. In addition there are subsidiary pressures on both sides that add to the total stress. In some cities strong rivalries among unions add to the difficulties faced by management. In others there are civil service commissions that are reluctant to share or reduce their historical role as protectors of employees.

The total situation shows further stress resulting from inflation, racial friction, and the generalized discontent of the current decade, so difficult to analyze satisfactorily and yet so obviously present. From this background the discussion moves to how local government employees are hired, promoted, paid, and directed.

CHAPTER THREE

Effect on Hiring, Promotion, Training, and Grievances

How employee unionism has changed "the merit system" or "civil service" depends on one's definition of these terms. In their earliest and narrowest meaning, they refer to a system in which citizens compete for government employment according to their qualifications for the jobs that are available. Examinations, often written ones, are used to evaluate the fitness of the candidates, and those with the highest scores are appointed first. "Civil service" in this sense has been little changed by employee unions. One finds a more profound effect on government management when civil service is defined more broadly—as a comprehensive personnel system that includes not only employee selection but also job classification, performance evaluation, training, discipline, resolution of grievances, layoffs, and pay and fringe benefits. Pay and fringes, which are of greatest current interest to unions, are discussed with classification in Chapter 4. The impact on promotions and grievance procedures is covered later in this chapter.

Hiring New Employees

"No effect" or "little effect" was the usual reply when interviewers in this study asked about the impact of unions on initial ap-

32

pointments. The answer was the same whether the person questioned was a union officer or a management official. In part this attitude results from long conditioned acceptance of the merit principle by union members. In larger part it results from the unions' concentration on other matters. It should not be inferred, however, that all unions accept the right of management to devise a civil service employment system or believe that management's judgments within such a system cannot be challenged. It is just that they spend most of their organizational energies challenging management's decisions in other areas.

When unions do take exception to hiring policies, they do so informally, concentrating on either the numbers to be employed, the standards to be used, or the methods to be followed. As to numbers, the real issue is likely to be fiscal policy, work assignment policy, or promotion policy, rather than employment policy. In New York and San Francisco, for example, the Social Service Employees Union (SSEU) has pressed for more generous financing and more aggressive recruitment as a means of keeping down the caseloads of welfare workers. On the other hand, unions oppose efforts to appoint new employees if they think the jobs should be filled through promotion. For example, the city of Dayton agreed, under pressure from the Dayton Public Service Union, to select truck drivers from among current city employees, not from outside.

EMPLOYMENT STANDARDS

Unions may try to change qualification requirements to benefit their members, or they may resist changes that they consider threatening. In the former case, there is usually a pay implication. If employees must meet higher standards of experience (as have building inspectors in Milwaukee or blue-collar craftsmen in San Francisco), higher pay can be justified for them. However, resistance to changes in qualification requirements is more common. The Uniformed Fire Fighters Association in New York successfully opposed a city proposal to drop the minimum height requirement for recruits below 5 feet 6 inches so that more Puerto Ricans could be employed. Police Local No. 224 in Tacoma objected to, but later accepted, a reduction of the minimum height from 5 feet

10 inches to 5 feet 9 inches. Unions may resist or favor the reduction of educational requirements, depending on how the change would affect their members. Recreation leaders in New York, for example, insisted on keeping the requirement of a college degree, while a San Francisco local of the Service Employees International Union (SEIU) favored eliminating educational requirements for custodial jobs.

Lowered employment standards are applied in "new careers" programs, in which cities employ and train disadvantaged citizens as an antipoverty measure. These programs, which are potentially stressful in union-management relations, are discussed below in the section on training.

SELECTION METHODS

In most of the cities the methods of screening job candidates are the same for initial hiring as for promotion. Unions are much more concerned with how promotions are made, but their attitudes also affect hiring practices. Generally they want to limit management's freedom to choose among candidates; and they want probationary periods (traditionally considered part of the selection process[1]) to be shortened.

Written civil service tests are viewed differently by different unions. They are favored by civil service associations and by police and fire unions, both of which draw their strength from long-term employees who are accustomed to the traditional civil service practices. Yet there are other unions, notably the American Federation of State, County, and Municipal Employees (AFSCME), that oppose written tests on the ground that they discriminate against poorly educated members of minority groups. Similar objections have been raised by other critics, who grant that pencil-and-paper tests are objective but point out that they measure verbal skills or "ability to take a test," neither of which may be related to job performance or to the pertinent qualifications of good candidates. Performance tests would be an acceptable alternative, but they are too expensive to administer to be used generally for civil service jobs.[2]

1. O. Glenn Stahl, *Public Personnel Administration* (6th ed., Harper & Row, 1971), pp. 143–44.
2. Robert H. Dicks, "Public Employment and the Disadvantaged: A Close, Hard

Under normal civil service procedures candidates are ranked in order of their examination scores, and the "appointing officer," usually the department head or someone acting for him, may choose any one of the top three (sometimes more) candidates. This latitude is allowed because no examining methods are perfect and there are personal attributes related to job success that examinations cannot measure. The appointing officer may also have some valid special reason for preferring one qualified candidate to another. Some cities, however, require that the candidate with the highest score be appointed. This "rule of one" contrasts with the more usual "rule of three" and is often favored by members of minority groups, who feel that a wider choice offers an opportunity for discrimination in appointments.[3] Unions generally prefer the rule of one and the supposedly objective imperfections of civil service examining procedures over choice by management with its possible subjective errors.

Union pressure on hiring practices has been effective in reducing the length of some probationary periods. Here again the objective is to limit management's discretion and to increase employees' security (hence, also union security). Bargaining resulted in shortening the probation period from six months to four in Dade County for positions not requiring an examination. Negotiations in Hartford cut the period from six months down to sixty days for blue-collar workers and to ninety days for clerical workers (with management having the right to extend this for sixty days more unless the union objects). The city management argues that this option is helpful in hiring members of minority groups since it gives them more time to show that they can do the work. The union, arguing for an even shorter probation period, says that the employer should be able to tell quickly whether employees are satisfactory. This union pressure actually could be helpful to management because shorter probation periods might be an incentive for more prompt and incisive evaluation of employee performance. One of the long-deplored failings of public personnel ad-

---

Look at Testing," *Good Government,* Vol. 86 (Winter 1969), pp. 1–8. See also William Scheuer, "Performance Testing in New Jersey," *Good Government,* Vol. 87 (Spring 1970), pp. 5–15.

3. Obviously this can work both ways. An appointing officer trying to "give an edge" to blacks in hiring may be inhibited by the rule of one. Some blacks urge wide-open selection from civil service lists.

ministration in the United States has been the neglect of opportunities to weed out marginal employees during probation.[4]

These indications of the unions' interest in hiring practices in public employment are exceptions, however. Generally they give little attention to this area. Employee organizations may well "move in" on public employment policy after higher priority interests are satisfied and as they progress toward union shop agreements. They can then be expected to press for a revision in employment standards and methods to favor their members or potential members and to keep out others.

Promotions

The effect of the unions on promotions has been modest, though greater than their effect on hiring practices. In all of the cities studied, the selection of employees for more responsible, more difficult, better paid jobs is controlled mainly by civil service laws and rules, although there are instances where promotions are governed by contract provisions. Unions' objectives on promotions typically include:

• Filling jobs above the usual entry levels only by promotion or by giving present employees some type of priority over outsiders;[5]

• Limiting the competition for promotion to employees in the organization unit where the job is located;

• Using specialized job content as material for promotion examinations so as to favor candidates who are already employed in the organization;

• Reducing the use of the subjective judgment of management in making promotions by opposing oral examinations and performance ratings—or by lowering the weight given to them;

• Making seniority a determining, or at least a very influential, factor, in selecting employees for promotion;

• Restricting management's freedom to select from among employees who have qualified for promotion.

---

4. Stahl, *Public Personnel Administration,* p. 144.

5. A closely related objective is the creation of new or revised positions so that new opportunities for promotion will be available. See the discussion of classification in Chap. 4.

Since these objectives can be achieved, at least in part, under civil service rules, changes in promotion procedures are not usually among the major bargaining or legislative goals of the unions. Also their objectives coincide to some extent with management's preferences. Even though a city personnel director may urge that jobs be filled by the best candidates, the system tends to favor insiders. The department head who must choose a new supervisory clerk or senior accountant normally selects an employee who knows the work and knows the other employees. The person chosen may well be the best possible candidate; even if he is not, choosing a senior employee from within the organization "keeps peace in the family" and is much easier than recruiting all over the city, the state, or even the nation.

These union objectives concerning promotions are old, familiar ones within most bureaucracies, even those without formal employee organizations. The difference is that nonunion pressures are exerted less formally. To the extent that these goals are already incorporated in civil service rules, the unions can simply show support for the status quo and pursue other aims. In this respect, then, unions are supporters of merit systems. There are, of course, variations among unions. Police, fire, and other professional unions and civil service associations tend to support established merit procedures. AFSCME is more resistant to civil service and more eager to use seniority as a promotion criterion.

This discussion of promotion procedures can be divided into two main parts: who are considered, and how choices are made.

FILLING JOBS ABOVE ENTRY LEVELS—WHO CAN COMPETE

In nearly all of the nineteen governments studied, the civil service commission or the personnel department decides whether a vacant job is to be filled by open competition or by promotion from within. Usually the latter method is favored, by such language as "as far as practicable, vacancies will be filled by promotion"—found in the laws or regulations of Dayton, Multnomah County, New York City, and Tacoma, for example.[6] In cases where

6. City of Dayton, *Civil Service Rules and Regulations* (revised 1968), p. 27; Owen Card (ed.), *Ordinance and Rules* (Multnomah County, Civil Service Commission, 1967), p. 5; *McKinney's Consolidated Laws of New York* (annotated), Vol. 9, *Civil Service Law*, sec. 52; Personnel Department, City of Tacoma, "Personnel Rules, City of Tacoma" (The Department, 1967; processed), p. 15.

jobs could be filled either by promotion *or* from outside, promotions may be given priority either by rule or by practice. Los Angeles County, Milwaukee, and New Orleans require that jobs be filled from promotion lists before open competitive lists can be drawn upon.[7] Unions, as was noted earlier, are strongly in favor of such provisions for obvious reasons. Two of the New York City union leaders interviewed were emphatic in defending promotion-first policies as an anti-patronage device. They said that it was better to promote qualified employees than to permit "politically minded city managements" to make provisional appointments of outsiders, in the absence of a list of persons who had passed examinations. New York City employee-relations policies provide for a special grievance appeal for employees who want to contest the holding of an open competitive examination instead of a promotion examination.[8]

Along with pressure for giving priority to promotion over open competition, goes pressure for narrowing the areas of competition, that is, promoting from within the department or other organizational unit. Although this pressure is not yet generally effective—rules in the governments studied generally call for city-wide competition—nevertheless, Los Angeles County and New York City give departmental promotion lists priority over city-wide rosters. More obvious exceptions to the general rule of city-wide promotion are found in fire and police departments, which are invariably closed services. There is absolutely no chance of a lieutenant's or captain's job being filled from outside the department unless there has been an impressive scandal or crushing political pressure.

There are other less exact ways of limiting the area of selection. Appointing officers may use their discretion under the "rule of three" to select from promotion lists only employees in their own departments. The qualifications for promotion—length and nature of service—or the technical content of a written examination or performance test may effectively limit competition to one department. Such use of management discretion to keep promotion areas

7. County of Los Angeles, Civil Service Commission, *Rules* (1969), Rules 8.05 and 12.03; City of Milwaukee, Board of City Service Commissioners, *Civil Service Manual* (City Hall, Milwaukee, 1967), p. 13; New Orleans Department of City Civil Service, "Rules of the Civil Service Commission, City of New Orleans" (1953; processed), p. 18.

8. New York City, Executive Order No. 52, "The Conduct of Labor Relations Between the City of New York and Its Employees," Sept. 29, 1967, sec. 8B.

narrow is usually encouraged by unions. Yet the viewpoints of unions on this matter tend to broaden with their membership. In Detroit, New York City, and San Francisco, unions were found to favor narrow promotional areas when they represented particular departments, and broader areas when they had members in more than one department. This distinction is particularly sharp in Detroit, where the Teamsters, with an interdepartmental bargaining unit, prefer city-wide competition for the higher-rated jobs; while AFSCME, with each of several locals having its own supplementary agreement with the city,[9] wants promotions restricted to its bargaining units.

The Detroit situation is unusual in that detailed promotion procedures have been negotiated and put into agreements. In other local governments the procedures are included in civil service rules, which unions may lobby to change. These Detroit settlements include the most detailed prescription of lines of promotion found in this study. The Teamsters' agreement permits promotion only from the next lower classification, for example, from truck driver to construction equipment operator to senior construction equipment operator.[10] Under the AFSCME supplementary pact in the Department of Public Works, a building cleaner may be promoted to comfort station matron, and a "laborer A" may be promoted to one of several specified jobs, such as garage attendant, street paver, or asphalt raker.[11] Like these examples, promotions in most of the agreements cover advancement to nonsupervisory but higher-rated jobs. An advance to "leadman or technical" positions is based on either a competitive civil service promotion examination or a test that is "advisory" to the department head.[12] Promotion to higher supervisory positions is left to regular civil service procedures. This is consistent with prevailing practice both in the other cities studied and in private industry, where the selection of

9. That is, supplementary to a master agreement with the AFSCME district council.

10. "Agreement between City of Detroit and the Michigan Conference of Teamsters" (Dec. 4, 1967; processed), p. 11.

11. City of Detroit, Labor Relations Bureau, "Catalog of Articles from Supplemental Agreements, 1968–69" (December 1968; processed), p. 42.

12. "Master Agreement Between City of Detroit and American Federation of State, County, and Municipal Employees, AFL-CIO, District Council 77" (October 1967; processed), p. 11.

foremen and higher supervisors is normally a management prerogative.[13]

Promotion in most of these cities is a matter of formal competition under civil service rules. The unions usually support or acquiesce in this approach. Admission to the promotion examination is normally limited to employees who have served for a certain time in lower jobs in the same or a related occupational series. A Dayton policeman, for example, must serve three years as a patrolman before he can take the examination for sergeant; another two years, for lieutenant; and another two, for captain. Such requirements may be of great interest to unions. When the International Association of Fire Fighters (IAFF) in Dade County asked that time-in-grade requirements be raised substantially, the fire chief opposed this effort to "load" the promotion process to favor men with longer service. Eventually they were able to recommend a compromise to the personnel division, as shown below (in numbers of years):

Promotion	Previous requirement	Requirement requested by union	Agreed requirement
Firefighter to lieutenant	2	5	3
Lieutenant to captain	2	5	3
Captain to chief fire officer	1	5	2

Eligibility for promotion may also depend on other criteria, such as the possession of a certificate (for example, a practical nurse or professional engineer license) or completion of a course in computer programming.

Promotions ordinarily are based on written tests, performance tests (or both), credits for seniority, and performance ratings. Less frequently oral tests are given. Each part of the total examination

13. Sumner H. Slichter, James J. Healy, and E. Robert Livernash, *The Impact of Collective Bargaining on Management* (Brookings Institution, 1960), pp. 188–98; Bureau of National Affairs, *Collective Bargaining Negotiations and Contracts* (1968), pp. 68–121.

has a prescribed weight, with the written test commonly being the predominant factor. Such test-mindedness represents partly a survival of a major aspect of the U.S. merit system heritage, partly a policy that is easy both for management and for some employee groups to accept. The judgment of department heads is to some extent guided by, and supported by, an instrument of apparent validity and possible predictive value. In reality, a truly valid test is very rarely found, that is, where there is statistical evidence that test scores correlate well with measures of job performance. Yet other selection devices, such as personal interviews, references from former employers, or seniority have not proven to be any more worthy of confidence.

Unions that support written tests do so because tests are considered more objective than oral examinations or performance ratings, which are regarded as ways of organizing management judgments. San Francisco police and fire unions succeeded a few years ago in getting a charter amendment adopted by referendum to prohibit the use of oral examinations in promotions. Milwaukee dealt with the union viewpoint differently by placing union members on the boards that conduct the oral examinations.

Unions also favor giving promotion credits for seniority—again because this is an objective measure. Management typically recognizes that such credits should be given but tries to set a limit, believing that after a certain length of time, continued tenure adds little or nothing to an employee's qualifications. For example, in Tacoma a competing employee gets one-fourth of a point for each full year of continuous service up to twenty years. Dade County (in the 1969 AFSCME agreement) gives one-half a point for each year of service up to ten years.

How Much Choice? When the examination process has been completed and the candidates are ranked on a list, the department head makes whatever choice is permitted him. In the localities studied he has free choice among the top three, with the following exceptions:[14] The rule of one is followed in Cincinnati, Dayton, Detroit, and Tacoma. Philadelphia follows the rule of two; however, it is customary for the police and fire departments there to select the candidate with the higher score. Among the localities

14. For simplicity, this ignores the effect of other legal and regulatory refinements, notably veterans' preference.

following the rule of three, in New York the police and fire departments usually choose the candidate with the highest score; in Boston and New Orleans the appointing officer must give his reasons if he does not select the top candidate; and in Wilmington there is pressure to choose the candidate with seniority. Dade County follows the rule of four. It is difficult to generalize from such an array of practices, except to note that there is a tendency to restrict management's area of choice.

Management really has more freedom than these limitations might imply. For one thing, the supervisor or department head may have promoted someone provisionally because there was no promotion list available. This person then often "has an edge" in retaining the better job when the competition is finally held; or, he may retain the job indefinitely if the civil service process is overburdened and the examination is never held. The SSEU in New York City has guarded against this possibility. Its contract with the city provides that, when 75 percent of the persons on the list have been appointed, the Department of Social Services will request the city's Civil Service Commission to give another promotional examination.[15]

Management may also be free to promote for another reason. A noncompetitive promotion may be made if the civil service authority concludes that competition is inappropriate in a particular situation. In some of these cases the promoted employee may be required to pass a qualifying examination.

Seniority in Union Agreements. Most of the union contracts in the local governments studied are silent on the subject of seniority in promotions. Many never mention seniority, while others treat it as only a basis for layoffs (which have been rare) or for shift and duty assignments (see Chapter 5). It may seem surprising that even aggressive unions in strong "union towns" like Milwaukee, New York, and Philadelphia are leaving promotions to the civil service procedures. There are two main reasons: first, civil service laws are controlling; and second, unions are concentrating their efforts on other objectives.

The major exception again is Detroit, where there is a wide range of provisions for determining which employee should be

15. Contract between the City of New York and the Department of Social Services and the Social Service Employees Union, Sept. 21, 1967, Article X.

promoted first. The agreements between the city and both the AFSCME and the Teamsters contain explicit provisions that the senior employee among those qualified and applying for higher-rated jobs will be promoted.[16] This requirement is less clear in the city's contract with the Detroit City Hospital Employees Union[17] and is expressed differently in the agreement with the Michigan Nurses Association. The latter allows the department head to follow seniority in choosing between nurses with equal qualifications. Ties between candidates are probably infrequent, however, because candidates for promotion are ranked on a weighted computation of their service ratings, nursing experience, training, length of service with the city, and length of employment in the facility.[18] In still another example of promotion policy, police agreements specifically identify promotion decisions as management prerogatives.[19]

Finally, the Detroit Fire Department uses a city charter provision, which calls for the promotion of the incumbent at the next lower level who has the greatest seniority—if he is qualified.[20] On one occasion when the department passed over the senior man, Local 344 of the IAFF filed suit on his behalf; however, the case did not come to judgment because the man retired. Of broader sig-

16. "Master Agreement Between City of Detroit and AFSCME, District Council 77" (October 1967), pp. 10–11; "Agreement Between City of Detroit and the Michigan Conference of Teamsters" (Dec. 4, 1967), p. 11.

17. Section 10A(1) of the agreement says:

In the event a promotional opening occurs within a section of the hospital division of the Health Department, the qualified candidate with the highest seniority who applies from within such section, shall be selected. However, in the event a qualified candidate cannot be secured in accordance with this provision, the Health Department shall select the qualified candidate with the highest seniority who applies.

An earlier section (8A) states that seniority "is established primarily to serve as a basis for the layoff and re-employment of employees." See "Agreement Between the City of Detroit and the Detroit City Hospital Employees Union, Local No. 1 for Herman Kiefer Hospital" (Aug. 22, 1967; processed), pp. 9–10.

18. "Agreement Between the City of Detroit and the Michigan Nurses Association and Its Affiliate, Economic Association of Registered Nurses, Unit I" (Dec. 7, 1967; processed), p. 19 and Schedule E.

19. "Agreement Between City of Detroit, Detroit Police Department, and Detroit Police Officers Association, Inc." (August 1967; processed), p. 5; and "Agreement Between City of Detroit and the Detroit Police Lieutenants' and Sergeants' Association" (1968; processed), appended Memorandum of Understanding.

20. Title 4, Chap. 15, Sec. 12.

nificance is a controversy that was ultimately decided by the state Labor Mediation Board. The Board of Fire Commissioners, with advice from the civil service commission staff, tried to establish the merit principle for promotion to higher ranks in the fire department by revising job specifications (to require graduation from high school and completion of certain training courses) and by directing the use of qualifying examinations. In one instance the most senior battalion chief was denied promotion because he failed the written examination, had no high school diploma, had not completed certain civil service courses, and had not demonstrated the type of leadership the fire commissioners felt was needed in top jobs. Although the board acknowledged that men of exceptional caliber were needed to run the department, it found that the city's changes in the promotion procedure were an unfair labor practice because they had not been bargained with the union.[21] However sound this decision may have been as a matter of labor relations, the result was a travesty of merit principles.

Conclusion. Methods of determining who can be considered for promotion and who will actually be promoted are matters of management prerogative in most cities and are usually governed by civil service provisions. City employees, both with and without unions, have been effective in narrowing areas of competition for promotion, increasing the weight of seniority in promotion examinations, and placing more reliance on written tests than on oral examinations and performance appraisals. Competitive civil service promotions are endorsed by civil service associations and police and fire unions, while the AFSCME and the Teamsters favor the seniority principle in union agreements. Experience in the city of Detroit suggests that, more and more, union contracts will provide for promotion on a seniority basis to nonsupervisory, higher-rated jobs. This development, however, will encounter reluctance from management and opposition from minority groups, whose members tend to lack seniority.

Unions are trying in general to narrow and inhibit management's freedom of choice in making promotions—a freedom that is

21. State of Michigan, Labor Mediation Board, Labor Relations Division, Case No. C67 F-58, *City of Detroit, Board of Fire Commissioners and Detroit Fire Fighters Association Local 344, IAFF,* April 17, 1968. (The Board is now called the Michigan Employment Relations Commission.) MERC made a similar finding in a 1970 case involving promotions to captaincies in the fire department training academy.

already limited by civil service provisions. This is a defensible viewpoint for two main reasons: (1) management's judgment is imperfect, being subject to error and favoritism, and (2) if employees have confidence in the promotion process, good morale is fostered, and grievances are reduced. The viewpoint is vulnerable, however, when it is evaluated against time-tested organizational principles. Management officials are chosen directly or indirectly by the citizens, who hold them responsible for the effective performance of public services. Anything that limits management's discretion, therefore, dilutes its responsibility and to that extent impairs the results of the democratic process. Yet this criticism can be refuted by taking another view of democracy. Public employees are a large and important part of the public—one of the more effective pressure groups. If they can affect the way in which the personnel system operates, this is simply one more manifestation of democracy.

It has already been noted that the influence of unions on promotions is limited thus far to promotions to the more desirable nonsupervisory jobs. If such promotions, based on seniority or on seniority plus other criteria, are made from a pool of qualified employees, the management traditionalist has little grounds for criticism. If ten truck loaders, for example, are qualified on the basis of training and tests to be drivers, why not promote the senior man? He can do the job, and choosing him is better for morale.

Promotion to supervisory jobs is another matter. There is no clear evidence as yet that seniority will replace civil service competition and management decisions in determining such promotions. However, this would be consistent with other union objectives and with the erosion that has already occurred in management prerogatives. It would also seriously weaken the fabric of urban government administration. The complex and urgent tasks of modern local government call for supervisors who have demonstrated enterprise, resourcefulness, planning skills, and capacity for leadership and who will enjoy the confidence of higher officials. It has already been noted that management's freedom to choose such supervisors has been curtailed by civil service limitations. The times call for further development of techniques by which management can select employees with the attributes needed to be excellent supervisors. They do not call for survival in a nonsupervisory job as a criterion.

Employee Training

Despite the obvious importance of well trained local government employees, this study's findings on the subject of employee training and education indicate little interest on the part of unions and considerable inactivity on the part of management. Training is a low-priority union objective, except where a few aggressive unions have tied it into promotions. On the management side, training is given as part of everyday supervision—to break in new employees, to correct errors, and to teach new methods. Yet there are relatively few formal courses or institutes. Training tends to get low-priority treatment because of other fiscal and administrative pressures and the still prevalent myth that government employees are fully qualified to perform their duties when they arrive on the job.

Some city departments have recognized their training needs better than others. Most police and fire departments run some sort of academy or initial training course. Recent public concern with law and order has led to increased efforts to provide supplementary training and education for police officers, although studies suggest that the need is enormous compared to the efforts to meet it.[22] Outside courses for police at city expense are provided, for example, by Dayton, Detroit, Hartford,[23] New York, and Wilmington. In city hospitals too, professional education is usually part of the nursing program, and staff development is an accepted, if underemphasized, part of the work of departments of social services. These are the most frequent kinds of training efforts in local governments, although some (Dade County, Detroit, and New York City) have broader programs of instruction. In most of the nineteen governments, training is a management enterprise, of little interest to unions.

There are exceptions, of course. The SSEU in New York, which runs its own training program to prepare caseworkers for promotion, bargained successfully for the city to provide paid leaves of

22. See Charles B. Saunders, Jr., *Upgrading the American Police: Education and Training for Better Law Enforcement* (Brookings Institution, 1970).

23. Hartford's tuition reimbursement program applies to other categories of employees too

absence for 350 workers for full-time study, under scholarships approved by the New York State Department of Social Services.[24] Nurses in Detroit city hospitals may, under their union's agreement with the city, be reimbursed up to $400 each fiscal year for courses taken.[25] Nurses in Boston also receive tuition reimbursements.

TRAINING FOR PROMOTION

Although training is now a secondary interest of the unions, enough examples were found of union-sponsored or union-supported upgrading programs to indicate that these will undoubtedly increase in number and scope because of their obvious advantages for union members, particularly those in low-paid categories.

Promotions in the Teamsters' bargaining unit in Detroit, referred to earlier, are made from a list of "pre-qualified trained employees"—employees trained under a program coordinated by the city civil service commission and developed in consultation with the union.[26] Similarly, the AFSCME district council in Cincinnati supported a project to train waste collectors to be truck drivers. A union-management program in Milwaukee to upgrade employees in the water and automobile maintenance departments dates back to 1950—before collective bargaining started there. Another union-supported program was offered by the New York City Department of Personnel to prepare building cleaners to be junior custodians, a line of promotion not open to them previously.

SPECIAL PROGRAMS FOR THE DISADVANTAGED

Urban governments, among other employers, cooperate in antipoverty programs to encourage the hiring and training of disadvantaged persons. The study revealed several instances of cities'

24. Contract between the City of New York and the Department of Social Services and the Social Service Employees Union, Sept. 21, 1967, Article VI.

25. "Agreement Between the City of Detroit and the Michigan Nurses Association" (Dec. 7, 1967), pp. 19–20.

26. "Agreement Between the City of Detroit and the Michigan Conference of Teamsters" (Dec. 4, 1967), p. 11; and Detroit Civil Service Commission, "Guidelines for Training Equipment Operators" (Nov. 12, 1968; processed).

participation in the Neighborhood Youth Corps for temporary and part-time work; the New Careers program, providing job ladders for city residents that will also help relieve occupational shortages; and the Work Incentive Program, offering at least part-time employment for relief recipients.[27] A few comparable programs were started by individual cities at their own initiative and expense. For example, interviewers for this study were told of the employment and training of the disadvantaged as community workers in Los Angeles County and New Castle County; the recruitment of social service and health aides from among welfare recipients in Hartford; the employment of housing authority tenants as caretakers and their training as maintenance men in New York and as police cadets in several cities; and the employment of the poor as hospital aides and street cleaners in Philadelphia. Many other examples could be cited.[28]

Early in 1969 the Department of Labor announced that some 1,000 hospital workers at Boston City, Cleveland Metropolitan General, and Milwaukee County hospitals would be trained for better jobs in a "ladder" program sponsored by AFSCME and financed by the federal government. The program provided five weeks of classroom work to improve basic educational skills, then an equal period of on-the-job training in technicians' skills—X-ray, dental, obstetrical, medical records, hematology, and others. Trainees received pay raises after completing each phase of the training.[29] (Milwaukee County Hospital dropped out after the preliminary stages of the program.)

These programs obviously have very positive values, yet they present problems for both city administrations and unions. Civil service standards must be loosened to accommodate the underemployed, either by making exceptions to the rules administratively or by passing legislation to place such programs outside the regu-

27. In addition, a new program called Public Service Careers created to secure "within merit principles, permanent employment and promotion chances for the disadvantaged in government agencies," and to stimulate upgrading of current employees, was developed after completion of our field research. This program, like the other mentioned here, is sponsored by the Manpower Administration of the U.S. Department of Labor. See National Civil Service League, News Release, Dec. 7, 1970.

28. No detailed research on such programs was attempted as part of this study.

29. Bureau of National Affairs, *Government Employee Relations Report*, No. 280 (Jan. 20, 1969), p. B-6-7.

lar civil service. Some of the beneficiaries progress to the point where they can meet normal civil service standards for regular jobs —particularly if written tests are not used or are given little weight. Yet the "batting average" is often low. Many of the case aide trainees in New York, for example, could not, even with substantial preparation, meet case aide qualification standards. Of 300 street cleaner trainees in Philadelphia, only 180 qualified for regular jobs.

Unions show a variety of attitudes toward these programs, ranging from enthusiastic sponsorship through wary acceptance, down to covert opposition. The cooperation of unions cannot be expected if they are not consulted in advance or if the beneficiaries of the new programs get preferred opportunities for training and promotion that are not available to union members.

Union resistance was avoided in Detroit when a civil service representative assured union leaders that the special program sponsored by the Mayor's Committee on Human Resources Development would not displace regular city employees. The unions agreed in writing not to file grievances over the assignment of work to the special trainees. Less harmonious was the situation at Philadelphia General Hospital, where the union "vetoed" a large majority of assignments proposed for members of the Neighborhood Youth Corps, holding that regular employees (who would become union members) should be given these appointments. In New York, trainees from the ghettos encountered a few "ugly incidents" with blue-collar workers in the traffic department, resistance to hiring on the part of union members in the parks department, and a questioning attitude from public health nurses on the use of "health guides" to make home visits.

Thus the situation is tangled, and patterns for the future are not clear. Unions are likely to display continued ambivalence in the absence of clear understandings, acceptable both to their members and to urban civil service officials, about how the trainees qualify for civil service status as well as for regular union membership.

The training function generally is thus still being treated as a stepchild of public personnel administration, and unions have done little to bring it further into the family at this time. An increasing tendency to incorporate training-for-promotion programs into union agreements can be expected.

Grievances and Discipline

Unlike training, grievances and discipline are topics of major interest to unions. The results of this interest, according to management officials, have been a slight increase in the number of grievances and a tendency to handle them more formally than in preunion days. There is a clear trend away from civil service grievance procedures to those set forth in union contracts, and arbitration by persons outside the government is replacing civil service decisions as the last stage in grievance procedures. Employee discipline, an area closely related to grievances, has felt less impact from unionism, but here again there is increased formalization, more union activity, and some use of third-party arbitration. Because of union resistance, managerial officials are more cautious about taking disciplinary action and more likely to consult with employee representatives.

GRIEVANCE PROCEDURES AND THEIR USE

Along with pay and fringe benefits, grievance procedures have become a leading topic in union contract negotiations. Detailed grievance provisions appear in union agreements obtained in all of the cities studied except St. Louis, which has no formal union agreements.[30]

Content. In most of these agreements, the question, "What is a grievance?" is answered broadly or vaguely, or sometimes not at all. A majority of the procedures deal with problems in interpreting or applying the agreements. This definition covers a wide area if contracts contain broadly stated provisions on management prerogatives, union security, hours, pay, fringe benefits, and working conditions. Some contracts use such terms as "any disputes" or "causes of dissatisfaction."

Despite this apparent breadth, a recent study by Begin, covering 304 union agreements for nonprofessional employees in federal, state, and local government agencies, finds that the scope of griev-

30. Two cities had only one union agreement each: New Orleans, in its sewerage and water board; and San Francisco, in Laguna Honda Hospital. Both include grievance procedures, and the San Francisco document incorporates the standard city procedure promulgated in March 1969. Los Angeles concluded agreements containing grievance procedures after the field research there had been completed.

ance procedures in the public service generally tends to be narrower than in private industry, although some local governments are exceptions to this.[31] The narrow scope in public sector agreements results mainly from the fact that public employees have another channel of appeal through civil service, which covers such matters as their performance ratings, the results of promotion examinations, the classification of their jobs, and most important of all, dismissals and other disciplinary actions. In the present book some of the agreements in which grievance procedures appear state that matters covered by civil service laws or rules are excepted; others are silent on this point. In the latter case the relative standings of civil service provisions and labor relations provisions have generally been determined by legal rulings.[32]

Civil service appeals and grievance appeals may be closely related. One employee might appeal to his city civil service commission, alleging that his assigned duties should be classified grade 22 rather than grade 20. Yet another employee may file a grievance under the union-negotiated grievance procedure, claiming that he worked temporarily on higher-rated duties but was not paid accordingly. In another instance an employee might appeal to the civil service commission on the grounds that he was given insufficient credit for his work experience in a promotional examination. Or he might appeal through the grievance procedure if his supervisor would not release him from duty to take a promotion examination. Despite such distinctions, the field studies revealed only one significant jurisdictional problem between civil service and union grievance appeals—the Detroit Civil Service Commission's objection to grievance appeals for out-of-classification work (see Chapter 4).

31. James P. Begin, "The Development and Operation of Grievance Procedures in Public Employment" (Ph.D. thesis, Purdue University, 1969), p. x. In addition to the analysis of 304 agreements, Begin reports on a survey of relevant literature and intensive case studies based on interviews in five cities: Dayton and Milwaukee (both included in this Brookings study), and Fort Wayne, Indianapolis, and Lansing. See also Joseph C. Ullman and James P. Begin, "The Structure and Scope of Appeals Procedures for Public Employees," *Industrial and Labor Relations Review,* Vol. 23 (April 1970), pp. 323–34.

32. Union agreements with the following governments have clauses assuring in some way the continuing effect of civil service laws or rules: Boston, Cincinnati, Dade County, Detroit, Hartford, Milwaukee, New Castle County, New Orleans, Philadelphia, and Tacoma. For a discussion of the legal basis of public service unionism, see Harry H. Wellington and Ralph K. Winter, Jr., *The Unions and the Cities* (Brookings Institution, 1971)

Not counting disciplinary matters (discussed below), the grievances filed under the negotiated procedures have most frequently concerned physical working conditions, assignments to particular shifts or locations, and interpretations of pay regulations.

Procedural Steps. Grievance procedures vary in detail not only from city to city but also from one contract to another within some of the cities; thus generalization is difficult. All the localities studied now have a formally announced, step-by-step plan for dealing with grievances. All but four (Cincinnati, New Orleans, St. Louis, and Tacoma) provide in contracts for arbitration, mediation, or recommendations by impartial persons at the final stage of the procedure. Perhaps most significant is the fact that in twelve of the nineteen governments, binding arbitration is stipulated[33]—clear evidence of a trend toward the making of final decisions by impartial third parties rather than by management (even an "independent" civil service commission). This finding is consistent with the results of Begin's analysis of contracts. He reports that 61 percent of the state and local contracts he studied provided some form of arbitration: 8 percent advisory arbitration, 51 percent binding arbitration, and 2 percent both types, depending on the issue being grieved.[34]

The usual grievance procedure steps and their most common variations are:

Usual grievance procedure steps	*Common variations*
1. Presentation to immediate supervisor in writing by employee or his representative	1. Oral presentation to immediate supervisor one step before written statement
2. Action by intermediate supervisor, division head, precinct commander, and so on	2. Action by head of department or agency
3. Action by head of department or agency	3. Action by top administrative official or city grievance committee
4. Action by top administrative officials, grievance committee, or civil service commission	4. Arbitration or final action by civil service commission or top management official
5. Arbitration	

33. Binghamton, Boston, Buffalo, Dade County, Dayton, Detroit, Hartford, Los Angeles County, Milwaukee, New Castle County, New York City, and Wilmington. Multnomah County provides for third party "mediation," but the "mediators" make "decisions."

34. Begin, "Development and Operation of Grievance Procedures," p. 39.

Grievance procedures almost invariably permit employees to be represented or accompanied by union officers at any stage.[35] In some agreements consultation between union and management officials is required at the third step. Prompt action is usually encouraged by placing time limits on decisions by both management and employees at each step.

Final Steps. In the cities where arbitration is used, generally a single arbitrator acceptable to both management and the union is appointed. Many agreements require the use of a designated source of impartial and qualified arbitrators, such as the Federal Mediation and Conciliation Service or the American Arbitration Association. An alternative plan, used in fire or police arbitration cases in Michigan local governments, provides for a three-member board of arbitration: one individual chosen by management, one by the union, and the third, who is chairman, by the other two. In the cities where arbitration is not authorized, management makes the final decision, after hearings and recommendations by a committee or a board.

It should not be inferred that unions are weak or that management is strong in cities where arbitration is not in effect. They are all strong public employee union towns except for New Orleans, but the unions have simply given higher priority to other objectives, notably pay. Undoubtedly more cities on the list will adopt arbitration. (It was included among union demands in Cincinnati in the 1969 negotiations.)

Arbitration Costs. Arbitration is a joint process. Management and unions agree on its scope and its procedures, and share in the selection of arbitrators. Since one of the parties might lack confidence in a process financed by the other, arbitration costs are shared in eleven of the twelve governments where arbitration is used. In the twelfth, Hartford, the state mediation board provides and pays for arbitration services. Yet even there the police contract calls for the union and management to share expenses.

Attitudes about Grievances. An overwhelming proportion of management officials interviewed showed no objection or resistance to the growth of negotiated grievance procedures and arbitration arrangements. Their attitude was neutral or willing, and some commented that supervisors were now making greater efforts to be fair.

35. In Cincinnati union representation starts at the second step.

Union activity might have been expected to result in a great increase in the numbers of grievances formally filed, since employees previously lacked opportunity or support for bringing out their problems. No statistical studies were made of the numbers of grievances filed and processed because the quantities are too small and variables too numerous to yield significant results, but interviewees were asked about the effect unions have had on the number of grievances. However, the usual answers were "no effect," "little change," or "just a few." Exceptions were Dayton, where the number approximately doubled in two years; Detroit, where an aggressive but inexperienced hospital workers' union filed hundreds of grievances; Milwaukee, which noted "'some increases" near the end of the period covered by the union agreement; and New York, where several department heads noted increases.

In his study Begin found that grievance rates in urban public service are low relative to those in private industry and that the reasons are difficult to pinpoint. Among the possible reasons are: limitations on the scope of collective bargaining, limitations on the definition of a grievance and on negotiated grievance procedures, the immature state of the collective bargaining relationship, a generally lower level of conflict, the presence of alternate channels to deal with employee discontent (civil service procedures), and inexperienced and untrained local union officials.[36] He suggests, however, that the number of grievances will rise as familiarity with the procedures increases and as the scope of what can be discussed widens.[37] Longitudinal studies on this point would be useful.

Regardless of the volume of business, the "safety valve" function of a grievance procedure was commented on by both management and unions. This was impressively demonstrated in San Francisco, where a work stoppage at the Laguna Honda Hospital unquestionably resulted from impediments to resolving grievances. The safety valve may exist in different forms, however. A Wilmington interviewee pointed out that in the days before union agreements a patronage-minded politician might settle a problem between an employee and his superiors. Another traditional alternative is of

36. Begin, "Development and Operation of Grievance Procedures," pp. 24–28, 230, 236–37.
37. *Ibid.*, pp. x, xi.

course an appeal to a civil service commission that is organizationally independent of other employing departments. Yet civil service commissioners are appointed by chief executives and are generally regarded by unions as part of "management," even though some of them may be biased toward employees' viewpoints. In both San Francisco and Dade County, for example, professional labor union officers hold positions on the civil service commission and personnel advisory board, respectively.

In any grievance procedure there are strong incentives on both sides for settling problems at early stages. Both want to maintain good working relationships and avoid trouble and expense. Union activity in the nineteen cities has not changed this. Only a handful of cases go to arbitration. Milwaukee, for example, reported seven decisions in a five-year period and seven cases pending; Dayton four decisions in four years, and five pending.[38] No cases had gone to arbitration in Binghamton or Philadelphia at the time of the research.

Despite the tensions and confrontations inherent in any grievance procedure, the general climate of the changes discussed above has been cooperative. In the cities where negotiated procedures and binding arbitration have been installed, management officials have accepted the changes, and the unions are gratified. In governments where civil service procedures are used, unions do not show any great urgency about making changes.

DISCIPLINARY ACTIONS

The impact of unions on formal disciplinary procedures has begun to be felt, but unions have made less progress on this front than in the grievance sector. The general disciplinary situation in the nineteen cities is complex and dynamic. For almost any assertion that can be made, there are cities, or unions within cities, that are exceptions.

Penalty Procedures. All of these local governments have some sort of civil service merit system to protect employees against arbitrary dismissal and lesser penalties. Under typical safeguards, the employee receives formal advance notice, has an opportunity to re-

38. *Ibid.*, p. 228.

ply, and may be given a formal hearing before the action is taken. He has the right to be assisted or represented in the proceeding. In addition, after the action is taken, he usually has the right to appeal to the civil service commission; if he wins his case, his penalty is reduced or withdrawn; if he was discharged or suspended, he is reinstated and given back pay.

However, this standard system is beginning to give way, under union pressures, to arrangements under which disciplinary actions are contested through negotiated grievance procedures leading to arbitration. The varying patterns in the nineteen governments are shown in Table 3. In all of these places under all of these procedures it is customary for employees to be represented by union officers or agents. (In San Francisco if an employee belongs to two employee organizations, it is common practice for both of them to support him at his hearing.)

Union pressure may also result in other procedural changes to increase the protection of employees and to reduce management's freedom to take disciplinary action. Employees of Los Angeles County formerly could appeal suspensions only if they were for thirty days or more. Under pressure from AFL-CIO locals and the Los Angeles County Employees Association, the criterion was successively reduced to fifteen, ten, and five days and now has been completely eliminated. At Laguna Honda Hospital in San Francisco the 1969 union agreement permits a delay of five days for investigation before a disciplinary suspension is imposed.[39] In Detroit several contracts protect employees from the effect of old misdeeds; disciplinary records sixteen months old (eighteen months in some contracts) are "washed out."

Impact of Unions on Discipline. The beginnings of a trend away from civil service appeal procedures and toward negotiated appeal procedures has been indicated above. There are other generalizations that can be drawn from the field studies. Union influence is felt long before formal actions are taken, and supervisors are well aware that hasty or unjust actions now will be contested. Most of the department heads interviewed took a positive view of this situation and said that this union pressure is good for both

39. Except when management clearly has to take immediate action, as in the case of an employee coming to work intoxicated.

TABLE 3. *Use of Negotiated Grievance Procedures and Arbitration in Resolving Contested Disciplinary Actions Taken by the Nineteen Local Governments Surveyed*

Government	Procedure
Binghamton	Decision through negotiated grievance procedure leading to arbitration for all employees except policemen.
Boston	Decision through negotiated grievance procedure leading to arbitration for employees covered by AFSCME and SEIU agreements; decision by civil service for other employees.
Hartford	Decision through negotiated grievance procedure leading to arbitration.
Multnomah County	Decision through negotiated grievance procedure leading to arbitration.
Wilmington	Decision through negotiated grievance procedure leading to arbitration, beginning at department-head step.
Buffalo	Decision by civil service body with advisory arbitration at the department-head step, subject to ultimate appeal to civil service commission or courts.
Detroit	Decision by civil service body with arbitration, but agreements differ among categories of employees as follows: for employees covered by AFSCME agreement, arbitration follows decision by civil service commission or mayor; for policemen, arbitration follows decision by trial board; for nurses, hospital employees and operating engineers, decision follows negotiated grievance procedure, beginning at the department-head step. Under state law, veterans can appeal directly to the mayor.
Milwaukee	Decision by civil service body with advisory arbitration to civil service commission.
New York	Decision by civil service body with, in general, advisory arbitration to department head; but employees with civil service status may appeal to civil service commission or courts.
All others surveyed[a]	Decision by civil service body without arbitration.

Source: Survey by authors.

a. Cincinnati, Dade County, Dayton, Los Angeles County, New Castle County, New Orleans, Philadelphia, St. Louis, San Francisco, and Tacoma.

employees and management. A minority view, sometimes supported by anecdotal proof, is that employees "get away with mur-
der" and that supervisors are afraid to enforce reasonable discipline. In one city two changes are symptomatic: garbage collectors
may now play cards during duty hours when they are not required
to work, and street repair crews are no longer required to wear
shirts on the job. The reader may decide for himself whether such
changes are good or bad.

General Quality of Relations

The typical urban government employee is recruited and examined through a civil service office, but after that most of his employment relationships involve his immediate supervisor or his department head, who is normally the official with personnel authority—the one who can hire, fire, promote, and discipline. The use of
supervisory authority by these officials is to some extent directed—
and inhibited—by civil service regulations and programs. Rules
and guides cover promotions, classifications, pay adjustments,
fringe benefits, training, and discipline. What happens then when
unions enter this picture?

First of all, supervisors acquire more guidance, as well as more
obstacles, in exercising their personnel responsibilities. The language of union agreements and the effect of informal union understandings are added to the previous complex of employment rules.
Where management is wise and effective, these added complexities
are not helpful for administration. Where management is arbitrary,
capricious, or uncertain, the union-sponsored safeguards are desirable. In cities where the personnel program is somewhat under-
developed (as in Binghamton or Boston) union provisions may fill
a partial vacuum.

Second, employee-management relationships tend to become
more formal and potentially more hostile. The employee who asks
for a promotion or a more favorable interpretation of a pay regulation or a change of shift is now more of an adversary, less of a co-
worker or subordinate—especially if he is accompanied by a stew-
ard or business agent. The supervisor or department head is well

aware that the union can go over his head, that it enjoys political influence with the city council, and that (in some cities) arbitration or even strikes hover in the background. He is therefore more tense and wary. He is also more careful, as was noted earlier. Unions tend to "sharpen up" management, as a Milwaukee official said.

Third, there is a lot of fumbling around on both sides when the union is newly recognized or when there is a new formal agreement. Union business agents, in this time of rapid expansion, are spread very thin. Stewards are untrained and inexperienced, unsure of what constitutes a real grievance, uncertain about what issues to take to union officers. Supervisors, equally naïve about dealing with unions, may be either too permissive or too strict. Both parties need to do a great deal more training of their representatives. Fortunately both sides generally recognize these problems of inexperience and have enough patience and good will to make up for the deficiencies.

CHAPTER FOUR

Effect on Classification, Pay, and Benefits

Unions have moved more deeply into pay and benefits than into other areas of management. They seem to have brought about impressive gains for their members, but it is not easy to prove that employees have been getting more through unions than they would otherwise have received.[1] Unions have certainly altered the *processes* of deciding what employees receive. In this chapter both the nature and the results of their pressures are examined, after a discussion of the job structures to which the pay changes relate.

Position Classification

Some system of arranging positions by occupation and within occupations according to difficulty, responsibility, and required qualifications is essential to any personnel system. In manufacturing, in the construction trades, and in commercial offices, hierarchies can be found in most occupations. The toolmaker outranks the machinist; the systems accountant is rated higher than the auditor of expense accounts. Similarly a traditional public personnel system is based on a position classification plan in which jobs are divided into various occupational series (such as civil engineering,

1. The effect of unionism on pay levels is the subject of another study in this series by Paul T. Hartman.

law enforcement, or accounting) and ranked within each series according to difficulty and responsibility (principal engineer, engineer; accountant III, II, I). Such a plan provides a basis for recruiting, examining, promoting, and training employees and, above all, for setting salary scales.

Classification plans usually include white-collar, service, public safety, and maintenance occupations. Employees in blue-collar trades and crafts (plumbers, carpenters, operating engineers, for example) may or may not be included in the classification plan, but in either event nothing is done to disturb the generally accepted duties in such jobs or their relationships to other blue-collar work.

In all of the nineteen governments, laws or ordinances require classification plans; and in all but two, the civil service commission or the personnel director is authorized to decide what jobs shall be placed in what class. The exceptions are Boston, where classification is handled by state civil service authorities, and Buffalo, where new jobs are classified by the budget director. In any of the cities, the creation of a new job class not previously authorized or budgeted calls for action by the budget office and the legislative body, as in the case of any new expenditure.

Classification plans are generally well accepted by unions in the cities and counties in this study. This is due only partly to the fact that classification is required by law and has long been used as a management technique; unions have never hesitated to try to change the laws and techniques they find objectionable. Rather, they recognize the need for a system of job organization and nomenclature; they do not find such a system to be a major obstacle to their progress; and they are understandably interested in the fact that the classification of a job determines its pay. To make classification more of an aid and less of an obstacle, unions are exerting three kinds of pressure, all related to increased pay for employees. They want some jobs assigned to higher pay grades, new jobs created to provide promotions, and higher "out-of-title" work properly compensated.

RE-EVALUATION TO HIGHER GRADES

The usual procedure for getting a job placed in another (usually higher) class is for a city department head to propose the change to the personnel staff, which then investigates and evaluates the proposal and makes a recommendation to the civil service commission, or personnel director, whichever has the authority to decide. Often too, the personnel staff may propose a change in order to have a fairer or more realistic arrangement of jobs in the city government. Behind either kind of proposal for change there is usually an employee (or group of employees) who wants a raise.

Unions have made this kind of pressure more visible and forceful. Union spokesmen deal directly with department heads and personnel officials to discuss reclassifications. They may also file formal appeals and support them in person at regular civil service commission proceedings. In some cities (Boston and Dayton), the classification of jobs is settled in the collective bargaining process, despite the view, long held in the public personnel profession, that classification analyses are technical matters, to be managed by trained staff experts. Even if the law reserves decisions to the civil service commission and thus prevents classifications from being determined through bargaining, a joint management-union recommendation can be made to the commission.

Representations by unions have created pressure to upgrade a variety of jobs in the cities and counties in this study: incinerator workers in New Orleans, orthopedic technicians in San Francisco, police matrons in Multnomah County, medical caseworkers in Los Angeles, and sanitarians in Dayton are a few examples.

NEW, HIGHER TITLES

Unions continually urge department heads and civil service commissions to set up new jobs to which employees could be promoted—a means of exit from "blind alley" positions. If this is done, costs go up, but there may be advantages to management, such as more effective supervision of workers, or retention of effective employees who would otherwise seek higher pay elsewhere. Nevertheless, the unions provide the motive power for such changes, and management often agrees either because of the benefits it derives or because it prefers to resist the unions on other issues. New York City provided good examples of this pressure to create new "target" job levels of senior caseworker, senior homemaker, and senior water plant operator. In Detroit a new supervisory level was created in the public health nursing field.

OUT-OF-TITLE WORK

Unions often defend the integrity of classification plans, demanding that employees be paid properly for temporary periods of work in higher-rated jobs. They point out that a laborer who works six hours as a truck driver at a laborer's pay is being exploited. Such problems are prevented or remedied by clauses in some union agreements. In Philadelphia, for example, the American Federation of State, County, and Municipal Employees' (AFSCME) agreement provides that the employee will be paid at the higher rate if he works four hours or more at the higher job. There are similar four-hour rules in Dayton and Detroit agreements. The time period varies in other places from any time at all in Buffalo, New Castle County, and Wilmington, up to three months in Binghamton.[2]

Difficulties in administering such provisions are reduced if there are explicit definitions of the content of each job. The Detroit Civil Service Commission and the Teamsters union worked together on a set of written guidelines for classifying equipment operation jobs, with illustrative duties and the types of equipment used set forth in detail.

Disagreements about out-of-title assignments are sometimes resolved through civil service procedures. Detroit again provides an example of an important policy change. The chief examiner and secretary of the municipal civil service commission maintained that out-of-title work controversies should be resolved by the commission under its classification authority, not through the bargained grievance procedure. The city went to court, requesting a declaratory judgment to this effect, but the court granted a defense motion (AFSCME, District Council 77, was the defendant) for dismissal, on the ground that no controversy was shown.[3] Under some Detroit union contracts this issue is still being disputed; under others, the commission's authority is recognized.

There is similar uncertainty in Milwaukee, where unions have

2. A complication should be kept in mind: if an employee is assigned for months to a higher level job, this may also be a circumvention of civil service rules on promotions. Hence, the rules may set a limit on the duration of such assignments.

3. Opinion, *City of Detroit, Civil Service Commission v. American Federation of State, County, and Municipal Employees, District Council 77;* Michigan Circuit Court for the County of Wayne, Case No. 124936, April 18, 1969.

presented classification problems under the grievance procedure, but the city has contended that such cases are not arbitrable but must be decided by the civil service commission. No such case has yet gone to arbitration. In Cincinnati and New York, however, field research disclosed examples of job assignment problems being handled under grievance procedures. There are also cases where no controversy occurred (probation workers in Los Angeles County did out-of-title work without extra pay), or where a controversy was resolved at the outset (Dade County lifeguards were asked to paint park benches during the slack swimming season; they complained; and management gave in).

CONCLUSION

The more aggressive union leaders would prefer to have classification decisions made through collective bargaining (for decisions on groups of jobs) and through grievance procedures (for individual disagreements on job levels). Yet even where classification is fully administered by management, it is generally accepted by unions. They believe in "equal pay for equal work" and its more cynical synonym, "don't let the other guys get more than you do." Their major energies, however, are devoted to bargaining or other forms of direct requests for increased pay.

Methods of Setting Pay

In a typical nonunion personnel system the personnel or civil service staff makes studies to determine what changes in pay rates are needed. They find out how much other employers, both public and private, are paying for various "benchmark" jobs (for example, accounting clerk, junior engineer, staff nurse, secretary, electronic technician). The staff then recommends changes in rates. After the recommendations have been approved by the personnel director (or civil service commission) and the chief executive, new rates are considered and enacted by the legislative body. During these processes, employees eager for pay increases make their influence felt in all kinds of informal ways, by bringing pressure to bear on personnel officials, supervisors, department heads, and the legislative body itself. Despite such pressures, the process is unilateral. Management initiates the studies, considers the factors involved, and makes decisions.

GOVERNMENTS NOT USING FORMAL BARGAINING

In all but three of the cities and counties (New Orleans, San Francisco, and St. Louis), this process has been displaced by formal collective bargaining (except for employees who are not members of bargaining units). Pay changes in New Orleans are determined by the civil service staff and commission, but a controversy arose with the Sewerage and Water Board, which does use collective bargaining. The civil service commission contended in early 1969 that all classified employees, including those in the Sewerage and Water Board, should be covered by a uniform pay plan. The board objected, and the matter went to court, where the civil service commission prevailed.

San Francisco and St. Louis, in both of which employees work under "meet and confer" laws without formal agreements at present, really carry on de facto bargaining. The unions are explicit and emphatic in their demands, which are presented in public hearings, supported by friendly politicians, and backed further by a demonstrated willingness to strike. Yet the process is not called bargaining, there is no provision for resolving an impasse, and the unions and the cities do not agree on a formal contract. Los Angeles County, operating under the same law as San Francisco, has concluded memoranda of understanding (in effect, agreements) with numerous bargaining units.

COLLECTIVE BARGAINING

A detailed analysis of the collective bargaining process is being made under another study in this series[4] and therefore will not be attempted here. A few high points are presented here, however, to show how greatly public personnel administration has changed.

Surveys and Other Preparations. The change starts before bargaining. Preparatory research and analysis are now undertaken by unions as well as by municipal personnel staffs. Bargainers from

4. By John F. Burton, Jr., and Arnold R. Weber.

the larger unions, not wanting to be outgunned by management's facts and figures, are typically well supplied with cost-of-living data and national, regional, and local salary information. In two of the cities studied, Philadelphia and Tacoma, the firemen's union had prepared elaborate illustrated brochures to state their case for higher pay. Other organizations—the Fraternal Order of Police in Wilmington and the Dayton Public Service Union, for example—make salary studies. In addition, many locals (especially those affiliated with AFSCME and the International Association of Fire Fighters [IAFF]) receive help from their national headquarters.

A unique situation was found in San Francisco, where the Service Employees International Union (SEIU) challenged some of the statistical work in the annual pay survey made by the San Francisco government. The union objected to an 11-to-1 weighting given to data from the public sector over that from the private sector and to management's practice of using figures from the 40th to the 80th percentile in summarizing its survey data. The union demanded that the entire spread of pay data be reported and that the city pay rates be comparable to the highest found elsewhere. Less ambitious, less well endowed unions do not make formal studies, but they have an acute awareness of pay levels in their regions for their members' occupations.

Pre-bargaining studies are shared in Buffalo, where management and unions exchange pay survey results, and in Cincinnati, where unions are invited to comment on the city's material and to submit data of their own. Elsewhere both parties disclose their information when they get to the bargaining table.

Other preparations are, of course, necessary on both sides. Management bargainers are aware of the fiscal limits within which they are expected to operate, and they are, it is hoped, well informed about the personnel situation in the various operating departments. On the other side, union bargainers have reached tentative conclusions of their own based on their estimates of what members want, what the survey data will justify, and what management will allow. In a few cases their ideas of what members want are obtained formally in meetings with the rank and file. However, much more frequently the bargainers are instructed only by the officers of the union, who presumably have a good idea of the members' wishes.

Productivity on the job, a key issue in private sector bargaining, was not a factor in any of the cities or counties in this study.

Relationship to Other Issues. In many instances, topics important to the basic relationship between management and employees —union security, the conduct of union business, and the grievance procedure—are settled when the first agreement is negotiated. In subsequent discussions, union demands may include supplementary noneconomic matters, but pay and fringe benefits—especially pay—receive much more attention; indeed, they are paramount issues for collective bargaining in all of the governments using this method. Any negotiations on hours of work or on conditions and calculation of premium pay are, of course, inseparable from bargaining on regular pay. In Detroit, where all negotiated matters except pay are covered in the city-union contracts, pay decisions are made a little later as part of the budgeting procedure. Unions receive memoranda stating what pay recommendations are being made to the mayor, but there is no formal pay contract.[5] Elsewhere pay is covered in the union agreements, often in the form of a detailed appendix.

Equity among Employee Groups. "Equal pay for equal work" is as important to both management and employees under collective bargaining as under traditional classification and pay-setting methods, but potentially more difficult to attain. If bargaining units are numerous and compete for employees in closely related occupations, differences in pay settlements may reflect differences in the strength of the unions more than differences in the work performed. Each union is perfectly willing to accept higher settlements for its own members but outraged if other unions get more. The problem is worse if different unions bargain and settle at different times, as they have in New York City. This leads to an alternating escalation of pay rates—sort of a "horse-race effect."

The problem has been solved in most of the cities studied by granting standard percentage pay increases or standard dollar increases to all employees. The latter is less desirable because higher paid supervisory employees will receive smaller percentage increases. Thus the gap between their pay and that of their employ-

---

5. In 1970, however, the unions signed stipulations that certain provisions of their contracts were subject to their acceptance of the pay package and economic fringe benefits offered by the city.

ees will narrow, rewarding them less for their higher skills and responsibilities. If management does not have a standard percentage increase for all employees, it should devise some systematic, rationalized plan of relationship between increases for different occupational groups. The problem of equity is also reduced if a large union bargains on behalf of its locals and achieves a fairly planned if not uniform settlement. This is done by AFSCME councils and by some Teamster unions.

Problems of equity become acute when occupations of strong and intimate concern to the public and to politicians are involved: policemen, firemen, garbage collectors, nurses. At the time when field research for this study was being conducted in Cincinnati, AFSCME members there struck briefly because the city had agreed to an increase of up to 9 percent for policemen and firemen but only 5 percent (later raised to 6) for the AFSCME employees. The strike was terminated within three days, and the disagreement was successfully mediated, with the union receiving a slight further increase in pay.[6] Another, far more damaging, strike over similar issues took place a year later. Garbage piled up, a sewage plant suspended operations, and striking union members conducted a lunch hour sit-in at a fashionable restaurant. The impasse finally ended with a pay increase of thirty cents an hour.

Policemen and firemen also received larger increases than did other organized employees in several other cities in 1968 and 1969 (see Tables 4 and 5, pages 76–77, below). A decision on a raise for Detroit police was made only after a "blue flu" strike had occurred, and the issue went to a state-appointed fact-finding panel, which functioned, in effect, as arbitrator. Interoccupational equity was strongly repudiated in the panel's report, which said that "it would be a disastrous policy to compel policemen to advance only in lockstep with all other City employees."[7]

Interoccupational pay equity is encouraged to a very modest extent by state law in Florida. The statute on collective bargaining

6. See W. Donald Heisel, "Anatomy of a Strike," *Public Personnel Review*, Vol. 30 (October 1969), pp. 226–32. Both this strike and the strike in Cincinnati the following year were complicated by racial issues.

7. Ronald W. Haughton, Charles C. Killingsworth, and Russell A. Smith, "Findings and Recommendations on Unresolved Economic and Other Issues" (Detroit Police Dispute Panel, Feb. 27, 1968; processed), p. 18.

for firefighters states that if unresolved issues go to advisory arbitration, the arbitrators shall consider (among other factors) prevailing rates in the building trades.[8]

Police-Fire Parity. A longstanding question of public personnel policy has been whether policemen and firemen should receive the same salaries. In the past policemen have been willing and eager to enjoy pay rates which were established largely as the result of efforts of politically influential firemen's organizations. More recently the situation has been reversed because of widespread concern with law and order issues and recognition of the great difficulty and responsibility of the police officer's job. Now the IAFF and its locals take vigorous exception to any examples of "disparity," that is, higher pay for policemen than for firemen.[9] Cities in which police-fire pay parity does not prevail pay policemen more because police jobs are evaluated as being more difficult or because problems of police recruitment and retention are more difficult, or both.[10]

On the whole, the firemen's organizations have been successful in winning or keeping parity with police salaries—and in some cases getting their own hours reduced, as reported below. Parity was the rule in all four counties and in twelve of the fifteen cities studied. By vote of the people the charters of Cincinnati and San Francisco contain references to this principle. The three exceptions are Binghamton, where police were raised 10 percent at a time (1969) when firemen were raised 5 percent;[11] Milwaukee,

8. State of Florida, Firefighters Bargaining Laws, sec. 9(1) (July 1967).

9. See discussion in Personnel Board of Jefferson County, Alabama, "Police and Fire Compensation and Related Issues in Public Safety Services" (1968; processed), pp. 73–76.

10. William F. Danielson, "Why Pay Policemen and Firemen the Same Salary?" *Public Personnel Review*, Vol. 25 (July 1964), pp. 158–64; Carl F. Lutz, "Relating Police and Fire Department Salaries," Personnel Brief 33 (Public Personnel Association, no date; processed); Carl F. Lutz, "Overcoming Obstacles to Professionalism," *The Police Chief*, Vol. 35 (September 1968), pp. 42–52; and Robert J. Grant and Paul Saenz, "The Police/Fire Parity Issue," *The Police Chief*, Vol. 35 (September 1968), pp. 53–59.

11. This issue went to a fact-finder, who recommended a 10 percent increase for firefighters and 5 percent for their officers. This would have caused distortion in the pay structure—a new fire lieutenant could have received less than a firefighter with long service—so the city decided on a general 5 percent increase. A strike of firefighters was threatened but did not take place.

where police pay moved ahead of fire rates in 1965 and has stayed ahead since then; and St. Louis, where the police are under the supervision of the governor of the state and are paid according to a different schedule.[12]

The parity issue is unusually complex in New York. Police-fire parity is well established, but three kinds of complications have arisen. First, other police and law enforcement unions demand and receive parity with the regular police: correctional officers, transit police, housing authority police, court officers, and court clerks. This pressure is resisted unsuccessfully by the regular police, who claim that they are "in the front lines." Second, the sanitationmen, who are "uniformed," have bargained and settled for about 90 percent of the police-fire pay rates. Third, there has been an escalating cycle of increases involving patrolmen, firefighters, and their supervisors. The city agreed with the police union that patrolmen's pay and police sergeants' pay would be on a ratio of 3.0 to 3.5, and with the fire union that firemen's and fire lieutenants' pay would be on a ratio of 3.0 to 3.9. A third agreement makes the problem mathematically insoluble: police sergeants and fire lieutenants shall be paid the same. When the police sergeants won a salary increase effective in December 1969, the patrolmen's union demanded a corresponding pay hike. The city refused, arguing that to comply would lead to a never-ending cycle of demands for raises, which would be fiscally impossible to grant. The union sued for breach of contract and damages and won an increase of $100 a month for some 25,000 policemen. The court concluded that only one round of increases was required, rejecting the city's contention that an administratively impossible succession of upward adjustments would follow.[13] It is not unduly pessimistic to expect other complex controversies in the future.

The widespread acceptance of parity is an important symptom of a management change resulting from union pressures. "Fairness" in pay as set by a management process means pay rates that

12. St. Louis voters on Sept. 15, 1970, approved a city charter amendment tying firemen's pay scales to those of police. The amendment was called unconstitutional in an analysis prepared by a law firm serving as consultant to the civil service commission. The firemen's union then announced its intention of filing suit to establish the validity of the amendment. (Bureau of National Affairs, *Government Employee Relations Report*, No. 377 [Nov. 30, 1970], p. B-14.)

13. BNA, *Government Employee Relations Report*, No. 362 (Aug. 17, 1970), pp. B-9 to B-11.

reflect job evaluation and market conditions (and some internal bureaucratic jockeying). "Fairness" in a collective bargaining sense means pay rates that reflect these same factors *plus* the unions' political and economic impacts on the government. Although job evaluation factors, personnel shortages, and prevailing rates are earnestly discussed in the bargaining process, they are less important to the final decision than is the sheer political power of the unions and their ability to tie up important public services.

PAY-SETTING THROUGH FORMULAS AND INDEXES

Some pay rates are set with little activity by either management or unions, but by reference to pay rates outside the local government. The most common example is the granting of prevailing wages of workers in the construction industry (for example, carpenters, operating engineers, sheet metal workers) to municipal employees in these categories. The U.S. Secretary of Labor establishes pay rates in various localities for workers engaged in federally financed construction, that is, work performed directly for the federal government or work undertaken by construction companies under contract to state or local agencies and funded in whole or in part by loans or grants from the federal government.

Some city governments pay the established rates for the occupations; but more frequently they pay a percentage of those rates. The percentage policy is adopted because governments can usually guarantee year-round work, while construction contractors are interrupted by bad weather, delays in receiving materials, gaps between jobs, and other problems. New York City pays 90 percent of the prevailing rates, which are determined by the city comptroller's staff, generally without bargaining and without action by the personnel department.[14] The employees receive the usual city employees' fringe benefits, which are probably more generous than those of the private contractors. In contrast, Dade County pays from 60 to 80 percent of prevailing wage rates, varying by the trade. And in San Francisco the strength of blue-collar unions is evident from the city's policy of paying 100 percent of

---

14. Certificated unions *may* bargain such rates with the city's office of labor relations, and a few have done so. Where agreement has been reached, the office of the comptroller has gone along.

prevailing rates, plus the city fringe benefits, plus a supplemental payment to compensate for certain fringe benefits that are available in private but not in city employment.

A good example of another type of pay-setting formula is found again in San Francisco. There the city charter allows the board of supervisors to set salaries of police patrolmen as high as, but not higher than, the highest patrolman salary paid by any California city with a population of over 100,000. The board may set lower salaries but has not done so. The charter provision was an amendment initiated and actively promoted by the police union.

While both of these methods reflect the strength of unions in looking out for their members' pay, they are used in lieu of further bargaining; thus both unions and management have relinquished some of their pay-setting freedom in establishing them.

A third type of pay-setting formula is added to, not substituted for, that determined through bargaining. Dayton's agreement with the Dayton Public Service Union provides for quarterly cost-of-living adjustments in bargained pay rates, that is, a change of one cent an hour for each 0.4 of a point change in the federal consumer price index.[15] Several of the Milwaukee agreements have similar provisions—for instance, in 1969, a change in wages of $1.0349 biweekly (or about 1.3 cents an hour) for each 1 point change in the index. Again, this plan reduces the discretion of both management and unions, but it helps achieve an agreed-upon objective without additional staff work or negotiations. Such escalator clauses are also found in the private sector, affecting over 2.6 million workers.[16]

PROBLEMS IN PAY STRUCTURES

An effective pay plan not only provides "equal pay for equal work" but also rates that are consistent with levels of authority and skill. Supervisors and department heads should usually earn substantially more than their subordinates; professional specialists,

15. Detroit adopted the same formula in a 1970 settlement, but with a maximum increase of fourteen cents an hour during any twelve-month period (*The Public Employee*, Vol. 35 [April 1970]).

16. Joseph E. Talbot, Jr., "An Analysis of Changes in Wages and Benefits During 1969," *Monthly Labor Review*, Vol. 93 (June 1970), pp. 49–50.

in view of their extensive education and specialized experience, should be paid at levels well above those of their less qualified associates; employees should have a real monetary incentive to seek advancement. These purposes would be poorly served by a compressed or distorted pay structure. During the field research for this study, urban officials were asked whether such a situation had indeed resulted from union pressures. Replies were negative on the whole, but there were several comments about the problem of blue-collar wages catching up with the salaries of supervisors or professional employees. Some laborers in Dade County, New York City, and Wilmington were reported to be making more money than their supervisors; some "nonprofessional engineers" in Detroit earn more than their professional associates. And in the San Francisco government, assistant civil engineers have applied for nonprofessional inspector jobs in order to receive higher pay.

Such difficulties arise from the fact that in governments, working-level pay is more responsive than supervisory-level pay to increases in the private sector. This responsiveness is due partly to bargaining and other forms of union influence, partly to sheer market pressures, partly to prevailing rate provisions, and in large measure to the political nature of the decision process. A city councilman has little to lose and something to gain by supporting pay increases for policemen and trash collectors. He has little to gain and possibly something to lose by supporting a pay raise for a department head from $18,000 to $22,000. Salary adjustments recommended by the mayor of Detroit in 1968 were planned to treat higher-paid employees fairly by granting them increases of up to 10 percent or $2,000, whichever was less.[17] But then the city council added ten cents an hour to the pay of all employees in the bargaining units and put a $1,200 limit on increases for executives, thus reducing the pay spread between workers and executives.

Three of the cities (Boston, Milwaukee, and New York) have found it necessary to establish special pay plans to solve these problems and to give adequate pay recognition to executives' responsibilities. These plans are of course quite separate from bargained pay provisions for union members.[18]

17. Except for executives in the police, fire, and nursing fields, who received a little more

18. See Robert C. Garnier and William Snell, "Management Pay in Milwaukee," *Public Personnel Review*, Vol. 31 (July 1970), pp. 203–07.

How Large Were the Raises?

It is hard to generalize about changes in pay rates over a two-year period in the nineteen governments studied. They all gave increases, but these increases varied in amount, in duration, and in method of computation. Further variations resulted from the effects of changes in hours of work, overtime pay rules, and fringe benefits, all of which will be discussed below.

For the most part, employees received increases that are reasonably related to increases in the cost of living and to increases in earnings of the general labor force. With few exceptions, municipal union pressures did not result in shocking or even surprising advances.[19]

PRICES AND EARNINGS IN GENERAL

The discussion that follows covers the trends first in the cost of living, then in general earnings, in government earnings, and in local government earnings, and finally in earnings in the particular nineteen governments studied.

Living costs and general earnings rose by roughly 5 percent and 6 percent, respectively. From 1967 to 1968 the consumer price index rose by 4.2 percent and from 1968 to 1969, by 5.4 percent.[20] Earnings went up more. Average weekly wages ("total nonagricultural private") rose by 5.8 percent from 1967 to 1968 and by 6.4 percent from 1968 to 1969.[21] Larger wage increases—amounting to 8 percent—were negotiated in major private sector agreements in 1969.[22] According to the Bureau of Labor Statistics, white-collar pay in private industry advanced 5.4 percent from mid-1967 to mid-1968, and 5.7 percent from June 1968 to June 1969.[23]

Government pay rates generally advanced more, usually because a need to catch up with the private sector was demonstrated. Un-

19. The Hartman study, mentioned in note 1, above, mathematically relates pay changes to unionism.

20. Computed from annual averages, *Monthly Labor Review*, Vol. 93 (August 1970), p. 112.

21. *Ibid.*, p. 107.

22. Talbot, "An Analysis of Changes," p. 46.

23. U.S. Bureau of Labor Statistics, "News," USDL 10-864, Dec. 9, 1969, p. 2.

der the federal law requiring that salaries be comparable to those in the private sector, salaried federal employees received an average 4.9 percent increase, effective July 1, 1968, and an average 9.1 percent a year later.[24] There was a further raise of 6 percent on April 15, 1970, retroactive to December 27, 1969.[25] Average earnings of state and local government employees rose 7.8 percent from 1967 to 1968 and 6.6 percent during the next year.[26]

Firefighters and police patrolmen received more, about 10 percent in 1968–69, according to a Bureau of Labor Statistics survey of cities with populations of 100,000 or more. Their increases over the two years were as follows (in percent):[27]

Fiscal year	In minimum annual scales	In maximum annual scales
1967–68	8.4	6.9
1968–69	10.2	10.3

PAY INCREASES IN THE NINETEEN GOVERNMENTS

With simplified versions of these figures as benchmarks—6 percent a year in the work force generally, 7 to 8 percent in local governments, and 8 to 10 percent for policemen and firemen—the 1968 and 1969 increases in each of the nineteen governments can be summarized (see Tables 4 and 5). The percentages are simplified approximations, and premium pay rates and fringe benefits are not included.

These gross figures show little that is surprising or out of line and little evidence that pressure from employee unions is driving up pay rates. The major cause appears to be supply and demand in the labor market:[28] Governments are directly affected by the market for employees in categories in which they compete with private

24. Executive Orders 11413, June 11, 1968, and 11474, June 16, 1969; BNA, *Government Employee Relations Report*, No. 249 (June 17, 1968), p. A-1, and No. 302 (June 23, 1969), p. A-10.

25. *Government Employee Relations Report*, No. 345 (April 20, 1970), p. A-4.

26. Computed from U.S. Bureau of the Census, *Public Employment in 1969* (1970), and two preceding issues, Tables 6.

27. Arnold Strasser, "Police and Firemen's Salary Trends," *Monthly Labor Review*, Vol. 92 (August 1969), p. 62.

28. See a discussion of this point in Richard Armstrong, "Labor 1970: Angry, Aggressive, Acquisitive," *Fortune*, Vol. 80 (October 1969), p. 144. See also George L. Perry, *Unemployment, Money Wage Rates, and Inflation* (M.I.T. Press, 1966).

TABLE 4. *Pay Increases Granted by Those Governments among the Nineteen Surveyed That Did Not Use Collective Bargaining, Calendar Years 1968 and 1969*

In percent, except where otherwise noted

Government	Year	Increases for employees other than policemen and firemen[a]	Increases for policemen and firemen[a]
Los Angeles County	1968	6.2 (average)	5.5
	1969	6.1 (average)	5.5
New Orleans	1968	5–7	6
	1969	7	3.5
St. Louis	1968	5 (10 for medical employees)	7–8
	1969	5, plus $13.65 biweekly (total of about 10 percent for employees earning $7,000 a year)	8 for policemen; 5 for firemen
San Francisco	1968	7.9 (average)	5
	1969	5	12

Sources: Interviews with, and records supplied by, officials in the cities and counties studied.
a. Fiscal years vary among the governments, as do the effective dates of pay increases. These figures denote increases granted during calendar years 1968 and 1969.

TABLE 5. *Pay Increases Granted by Those Governments among the Nineteen Surveyed That Used Collective Bargaining, Calendar Years 1968 and 1969*

In percent, except where otherwise noted

Government	Year	Increases for employees other than policemen and firemen[a]	Increases for policemen and firemen[a]
Binghamton	1968	b	b
	1969	5	10 for policemen; 5 for firemen
Boston	1968	6	14 for policemen; 8 for firemen (effective Jan. 1, 1969)
	1969	4.5 (March); 7 (September)[c]	10 for policemen; 6 for firemen
Buffalo	1968	15	20
	1969	5.5 (effective Jan. 1, 1969)	5.5
Cincinnati	1968	2 (cost of living increase)	2 (cost of living increase)
	1969	6	9
Dade County	1968	5–10 ($250 a year, plus 2 percent of base pay)	12
	1969	5–10 ($500 a year for employees generally; 60 cents an hour for waste division employees; 10–15 percent for professionals)	9 (13 percent for police lieutenants and above)

TABLE 5 (*continued*)

Government	Year	Increases for employees other than policemen and firemanᵃ	Increases for policemen and firemenᵃ
Dayton	1968	5	⎫
	1969	7 (19 cents an hour, plus cost of living increase)	⎬12.5 over two years
			⎭
Detroit	1968	14 (there had been no increase in 1967)	19 (there had been no increase in 1967)
	1969	9	5
Hartford	1968	6.4 (7 percent deferred for one month)	12.9 (10 percent at beginning of fiscal year, plus 7 percent deferred 7 months)
	1969	5	5
Milwaukee	1968	3 (or 10 cents an hour, whichever was greater)	None for policemen; $300 for firemen
	1969	25 cents an hour effective in January; 10 cents an hour effective in July	$500 a year for policemen; $400 a year for firemen
Multnomah County	1968	About 6 ($35 a month)	About 6 ($35 a month)
	1969	7	About 8.5
New Castle County	1968	7	7
	1969	7	7
New York	1968	⎫Wide variations, but roughly	11
	1969	⎭ 20 over two years	5
Philadelphia	1968	8	⎫
	1969	$600 (10 percent or less)	⎬About 20 over two years
Wilmington	1968	7.5	7.5
	1969	About 8 ($3 an hour)	About 8 ($3 an hour)

Sources: Interviews with, and records supplied by, officials in the cities and counties studied.

a. Fiscal years vary among the governments, as do the effective dates of pay increases. These figures denote increases granted during calendar years 1968 and 1969.

b. The city corporation counsel said that a city-wide classification and wage survey was conducted by the New York State civil service department and that resulting wage changes took effect in 1968 but that it was impossible to determine percentage increases for individual groups of employees.

c. A three-year contract granting one and one-half pay steps (just under 7 percent) each year became effective in September.

employers. They are also under political and internal pressure (and part of such pressure is from organized employees) to conform to pay rates in the private sector.

Pay increases are hard to finance (see Chapter 6), and one can speculate that, without union pressures, urban governments in fiscal distress would resist them; but there is no clear evidence of such a tendency. Detroit gave no increases in 1967 despite the presence of strong unions, but it made up for this with a 14 percent increase the following year. Cincinnati gave only a 2 percent cost-of-living increase in 1968,[29] but gave a 6 percent increase in 1969.

Thus the general picture is clear. So far, in most of these cities, unions are not forcing pay rates to levels significantly above general patterns. Yet there are impressive instances where unions have used work stoppages or other aggressive actions to get higher wage settlements for their bargaining units than other employees have received. In all these situations the employees were working in fields important to the public health and safety. Such actions not only result in unplanned increases and new fiscal problems but also disrupt community services and municipal administration.[30]

A notable example has already been mentioned: the Detroit police impasse in 1967. The Detroit Police Officers' Association requested a maximum base salary of $9,000 for 1966–67, an increase of $1,665. Instead they (and the firemen) received a raise of $1,000, $688 more than other employees. In continuing negotiations in late 1966, they requested a further increase for the then current fiscal year, plus fringe benefits, and an increase to $10,000 maximum base pay for fiscal year 1967–68. The city refused further increases for 1966–67 and then gave none to any employees for 1967–68. Subsequently the police staged a "ticket slowdown," which resulted in some disciplinary actions, and then had a "blue flu" epidemic—excessive sick calls. This resulted in a court injunction, intervention by a citizens' committee, and ultimately the appointment of a fact-finding dispute panel. After four months of hearings and briefings, this body found in favor of the $10,000 request, overriding the city's claim of inability to pay, but refused to

29. There had been a more substantial increase in 1967 and agreement that there would be no further increase for two years. Management, however, initiated the 2 percent increase because of the rising cost of living and rising comparative pay rates.

30. John F. Burton, Jr., and Arnold R. Weber in their Brookings study of collective bargaining in the public sector will discuss impasse resolution. See also Harry H. Wellington and Ralph K. Winter, Jr., *The Unions and the Cities* (Brookings Institution, 1971).

make this and other increases retroactive.[31] Another example from Detroit: in the following year (1968–69), when employees generally received a 6 percent increase, hospital nurses, threatening to resign, received 12 percent plus a $300 bonus for work in one hospital where there is a large emergency workload.

Many examples can be given from other local governments. The salaries of Dade County trash collectors rose 8 percent after a strike in 1968, though other employees received increases of 2 percent plus $250 a year—which would be a total of 6.2 percent for a $6,000 employee.[32] On the other hand, garbage collectors in Milwaukee struck for six days in 1969 but gained no greater pay increase than did other employees. However, after a disastrous strike in 1968, New York City sanitationmen received a two-year increase of roughly 20 percent—a higher raise than the city was prepared to give, which resulted in a larger-than-planned increase for policemen and firemen as well. Obviously, pressure tactics do pay off and can be expected to be used by the unions that have the necessary political strength.[33]

Furthermore, it can hurt not to belong to a union. Examples of this were found in Wilmington and Buffalo, where in 1968 and 1969, respectively, cost-of-living raises were not given to unrepresented employees, though they were granted to union members.

Hours of Work

Bargaining and other union-management discussions in the nineteen governments have had little to do with hours of work, except for firefighters. For other employees the length of the standard work week, whether it was 40, or 35 hours, rarely became an issue.

31. For details see Haughton, Killingsworth, and Smith, "Findings and Recommendations on Unresolved Economic and Other Issues." Michigan has since enacted compulsory, binding arbitration to be used in police and firemen's bargaining impasses. An arbitration board in 1970 gave fifth-year patrolmen an increase that brought their salaries to $12,000, leading to layoffs and increased working hours for other employees (later rescinded by court order). BNA, *Government Employee Relations Report*, No. 361 (Aug. 10, 1970), p. B-9, and No. 363 (Aug. 24, 1970), p. B-14.

32. The trash collectors gained even more after a two-day wildcat strike in 1970. BNA, *Government Employee Relations Report*, No. 370 (Oct. 12, 1970), p. B-12.

33. Note again, however, that the number of strikes is small compared to the number of agreements successfully concluded. See Chap. 2, pp. 18–19, and note 8.

An exception was the problem of shortened summer hours in New York City. Soon after John Lindsay became mayor in 1966 he tried to stop the city practice of cutting an hour off the working day during the summer months. The unions objected that the practice was so well established that it was an accepted condition of employment; they won their point. A comparable problem came up in Detroit in 1970 when Mayor Roman S. Gribbs asked some eight thousand city employees to work 40 hours instead of the regular 35, so that city services could be maintained despite fiscal stringencies. Union reactions were violently adverse and resulted in a court order that the mayor's directive be rescinded.[34]

Otherwise, direct union pressures to reduce hours were apparent mainly in the case of fire departments. In Boston this brought agreement to cut hours from 48 to 46 in 1970, to 44 in 1971, and to 42 in 1972. Hartford went from 56 to 48 in 1968 and will go to 42 in 1971; and Wilmington cut from 56 to 52 in 1967 and to 48 in 1971. In St. Louis, Los Angeles, Milwaukee, New Orleans, and New York (where the police workweek was also shortened),[35] varying reductions over different periods were reported. San Francisco agreed to reductions in mid-1970 just in time to avert a strike. All such changes are beneficial to the employees, but create problems for management. The firemen get more pay for each hour worked, and they have more time available to work at second jobs. On the other hand, management must re-plan shift assignments and provide additional manpower at higher total costs.

Overtime and Other Special Pay Arrangements

Under union pressure municipal governments have been liberalizing overtime rates and other forms of extra pay. Some of these changes have been bargained; others went into effect before formal negotiations were undertaken but were later put into union agreements. In either case it is difficult to know how much credit to give unions for the changes. Liberalization has been taking

---

34. BNA, *Government Employee Relations Report*, No. 363 (Aug. 24, 1970), p. B-14, and No. 365 (Sept. 7, 1970), p. B-16.

35. For several years New York police, who have an official 40-hour week, have worked 42 hours, receiving 2 hours' overtime pay.

place in the private sector also, and the labor market puts pressure on governments to conform. Still, unions have clearly achieved results through insistence and perseverance. Paid overtime is replacing compensatory time off in some cities, and time and a half is replacing straight time in others. Policemen and firemen are beginning to be paid at premium rates for overtime.[36] Differentials in pay for evening and night shifts have been introduced in some of the governments in this study and have been increased in others. In addition, employees called back to duty on their own time are being paid for two, three, or four hours, even if they work less than this—and generally at overtime rates. Examples of such changes are given in more detail in Appendix B.

These pay liberalizations, although beneficial to employees, lead to an increase in costs, in administrative difficulties, and in personnel controversies. As premium pay provisions become more generous and complex, supervisors and payroll officers must determine who is eligible for overtime or shift differentials under varying circumstances. Formal grievances are frequently filed. This is a substantial change from the practice of letting an employee choose a half day to take off because he worked last Saturday morning.

Some of these more generous premium pay arrangements have caused unforeseen administrative quirks. One city (which will not be named) provides four hours' minimum callback at time-and-a-half pay. A management official there said that he had good grounds for suspecting abuses in the sewer cleaning unit. Apparently the sewer cleaners had their friends call at night for emergency service to remove sewer stoppages so that the crew could get extra pay. The city planned to solve the problem by refusing to send out a crew unless a private plumber was first called by the householder and found trouble in the city's part of the sewer.

Hartford encountered a problem of broader scope. When the AFSCME received time and a half for overtime in its first contract, city officials made other changes in an effort to be fair to employees who were not members of bargaining units. Most blue-collar foremen were given a 5 percent differential plus straight time pay for overtime worked. This change won general acceptance. But an-

36. In the summer of 1970 the Professional Policemen's Protective Association (Milwaukee) warned that unless police received a federal guarantee of overtime pay, there would be a definite threat of a nationwide police strike. BNA, *Government Employee Relations Report*, No. 357 (July 13, 1970), pp. B-4, B-5.

other change—giving professional and managerial employees a 5 percent differential in lieu of overtime—was less favored. It was criticized by some department heads for various reasons: (1) many employees do not work overtime but get the 5 percent anyway; (2) others work so much overtime that the 5 percent is inadequate compensation for what they do; and (3) when all such employees receive the differential, it seems unfair to ask some, but not others, to work overtime. The city would have been spared these difficulties if it had followed the more conventional practice of drawing a line above which employees are considered executives and are not paid overtime and below which those who work overtime receive extra pay.[37] Nevertheless the new system has come to be generally accepted by Hartford executives.

Union attention to pay levels is overwhelmingly devoted to regular pay rates, and after that to overtime and shift differentials. Only sporadic attention is given to longevity pay and hazard pay, and virtually none to merit pay.

There has been little negotiation on hazard pay in the nineteen localities, but enough to suggest that there will be more activity in the future after higher priority desires are satisfied. As a result of union pressure Dade County increased extra pay for the police bomb squad from $10 to $50 per month and provided additional compensation for window washers. Los Angeles County nurses get extra pay for serving in psychiatric and communicable disease wards, and nurses in San Francisco city hospitals have won some complex and beneficial special pay provisions. In addition to base pay, they get 2.5 percent extra if on psychiatric assignment, 5 percent if assigned to emergency service, 5 percent if on ward duty, 10 percent for night shift work, and $20 a month if in a communicable disease area. Thus employees gain, and computers are needed to figure payrolls.

Fringe Benefits

As in the case of pay, fringe benefit patterns also vary, and generalization is difficult. Benefits are being liberalized and are rea-

---

37. This would have the drawback, however, of narrowing the salary differences between supervisors and subordinates, a problem noted on pp. 72 and 73, above.

sonably in line with practices in the private sector. The gains cannot be clearly credited to unions because market pressures are felt in this area too, and generally governments were generous with fringes long before private businesses were. However, fringe benefits have become more liberal under union pressures, as well as other pressures, and costs of government have risen some more. The gains consist of longer vacations, additional holidays, slightly more generous sick leave, larger government payments for health benefits and group life insurance, and more generous pensions. Thus urban public administrators find that employees work fewer hours annually and are given more incentive and opportunity to retire early, all at a higher cost. These management disadvantages are offset to some degree by the increased attractiveness of municipal employment and (presumably) by the efficient performance of secure and satisfied employees.

VACATIONS AND HOLIDAYS

Graduated leave plans (that is, longer leaves for employees with longer service) are common in the governments studied, with vacations of four weeks or more customary for the more senior employees. This is also true in private industry, according to a 1969 study by the U.S. Bureau of Labor Statistics.[38] A further comparison of the BLS data with information from the nineteen local governments shows that annual leave policies in the private and public sectors are fairly consistent[39] (see Appendix B for examples).[40]

Additional holidays are not a major union objective, but they often turn up in the first list of demands. They have been granted

38. U.S. Bureau of Labor Statistics, *Major Collective Bargaining Agreements: Paid Vacation and Holiday Provisions*, Bulletin 1425-9 (1969), p. 5. "Benefits of four weeks or more were found in almost 73 per cent of the more recent [collective bargaining] agreements containing graduated plans. . . . The study shows that vacation allowances have also continued to be liberalized beyond the prevailing four weeks."

39. *Ibid.*, pp. 4–7.

40. Examples of fringe benefits, both in this chapter and in Appendix B, are necessarily oversimplified. They apply to "employees generally," in the more common unionized blue-collar and white-collar occupations. Different fringe benefits in many cities are enjoyed by policemen, firemen, hourly rate employees, hospital workers, and others.

in a few cities: each employee's birthday in Dayton; a half day each before Christmas and New Year's Day in Dade County and Detroit; both Lincoln's and Washington's birthdays in Hartford (formerly only one of these, whichever fell on or closer to a Friday or Monday); and one more holiday in New York (the result of guaranteeing a day off if the actual holiday falls on a Saturday).

In a few instances management has tried to swim against the tide but has not always been successful. New Orleans (a noncollective bargaining city) has eliminated two holidays: Confederate Memorial Day and Huey Long's birthday.

SICK LEAVE

Paid sick leave is of lesser interest, and unions have brought about either no change or little change in the majority of the nineteen localities. As an exception, uniformed employees in New York can now be given unlimited sick leave if it is needed as a result of injuries received while on the job. Four governments (Dayton, Detroit, Milwaukee, and Multnomah County) have increased the total amount of sick leave that may be accumulated. Philadelphia management tried in vain to reduce the amount of sick leave employees could accumulate. (They can save up as much as 200 days and be paid at retirement for 30 percent of the unused accumulation.)

St. Louis had an unusual system, now changed under union pressure. Sick leave was granted without limit at the discretion of the supervisor, and there was no system of accumulation. The city has now agreed that, in cases of genuine illness, the supervisor may not refuse sick leave up to the amount an employee would have accumulated if he were earning 5 hours of sick leave biweekly ($16\frac{1}{4}$ days a year) with a maxium accumulation of 720 hours. The supervisor may grant more than this if he wishes. This is another example of the unions' desire to curtail managerial discretion and to rely instead on rules and formulas.

HEALTH BENEFITS AND LIFE INSURANCE

Negotiations or discussions in about half of the cities dealt with hospital and medical insurance and group life insurance—always in the direction of liberalization. Under union pressure, Dayton, Hartford,[41] Milwaukee, New Castle County, and Wilmington have in recent years moved to full government financing of hospital and medical insurance premiums[42] for both the employee and his family. New York, which already provided this benefit, began giving employees a choice of three plans. Philadelphia in 1969 raised the city's contribution to established medical plans by 20 percent. Boston, limited by city legislation to paying only half, is now permitted by a new state law to finance a larger percentage and will presumably do so. And Cincinnati, which already paid for hospital and surgical insurance, agreed in 1969 to fully paid major medical insurance.

At the same time those governments that pay for group life insurance have been increasingly generous (see Appendix B for examples).

RETIREMENT

Pension systems are becoming more generous too, as to both eligibility for retirement and size of annuities. These changes require more effort on the part of both unions and management than do other fringe benefit liberalizations. Since municipal retirement is governed in detail by state laws in New York, Ohio,[43] and Delaware, unions and local government officials must meet with members and committees of the state legislatures. In Detroit and San Francisco, specific provisions of the retirement systems are in the charters, which can be amended only by vote of the people, who have to be convinced. Another source of difficulty is the sheer complexity of retirement problems—a compound of personnel policy, actuarial computations, and fiscal impact.

Union influence has helped to overcome these obstacles both in starting and in liberalizing retirement systems. Unions lobbied strongly, for example, for the establishment of a retirement plan in St. Louis. And when the first union contract was negotiated in

41. For the AFSCME general employee contract. Provisions differ in the police and fire agreements.

42. The usual "Blue Cross-Blue Shield" arrangement or its equivalent.

43. Except for Cincinnati, which has its own pension system antedating the state legislation.

Buffalo under the state public employment labor relations law (the "Taylor law"), it included a provision that the city would support a "1/60" noncontributory retirement plan.[44] Dade County, which participates by law in a state operated and controlled retirement system, began paying half of its employees' 6 percent contribution to the retirement plan in 1968. The unions wanted an equivalent pay increase, but the county manager personally took a strong hand in the bargaining and won this point. As a result, employees get more take-home pay than they would have with the pay increase.

Inquiries about recent changes in pension plans that are attributable to union pressure revealed a variety of liberalizing steps (see Appendix B for examples).

OTHER FRINGES

As unions achieve their primary objectives—union security, increased pay, and the benefits discussed above—they can be expected to seek other fringes in order to maintain the interest and confidence of their members. This is evident from experience in two of the stronger "union towns," Detroit and New York. The Teamsters union in Detroit asked for a pay increase of twenty cents an hour, plus seven cents an hour to pay for union-sponsored optical and dental care and two cents an hour for supplemental pension benefits. City bargainers refused because they did not want one employee group to have benefits not granted to others and offered instead a straight pay increase. The union unsuccessfully contested this, labeling it a refusal to bargain.

Extra benefits in New York are provided by insurance and welfare funds, to which the city contributes but over which it has limited authority. The city cannot determine what the money will be spent for but can audit for irregularities, as it did in the case of alleged improprieties in the management of funds of the Patrolmen's Benevolent Association.[45] Annuity funds maintained by

44. To oversimplify, this means that pensions are computed by multiplying the employee's salary by one-sixtieth times his number of years of service (for example, $10,000 salary $\times$ 1/60 $\times$ 33 years = $5,500 pension).

45. David Burnham, *New York Times*, March 27, 1970.

the police, fire, and sanitationmen's unions receive one dollar per working day per employee.[46] These unions also have welfare funds that finance a variety of supplementary medical services, and, in the case of the sanitationmen, scholarships, recreation facilities, and emergency loans. The city pays $190 per year per man into the patrolmen's fund, $130 into the firemen's, and $219 into the sanitationmen's. There are also payments of $125 for elevator operators, $105 for Housing Authority employees, and $85 for caseworkers. Such funds are not uncommon in private industry; the Teamsters, Mine Workers, and Garment Workers unions have had them for many years. This development in government is an important policy precedent. Unions not only are getting increased benefits but benefits that they can control—another evidence of the trend away from management-controlled personnel policy and another cause of increased costs.

FURTHER LIBERALIZATIONS

Two major AFSCME settlements that were concluded after the field research for this study was completed suggest that the trend to more generous fringe benefits is accelerating. The first, with Detroit, more than triples the benefit in case of death while on duty (from $750 to $2,500); gives the employee and his family comprehensive eye care; provides an additional holiday; initiates an income protection plan—up to $66\frac{2}{3}$ percent of take home pay for up to three years after sick leave is exhausted; and liberalizes holiday pay, shift differentials, and automobile allowances.[47] A subsequent agreement in New York boosted pensions: retirement in twenty years at half pay, plus 2.5 percent of salary for each year beyond twenty, to a maximum of 100 percent for forty years. Also granted were increases in health and security fund payments, better premium pay, a more liberal maternity leave benefit, and increased meal and automobile allowances.[48]

---

46. For firemen, actually one dollar per nine-hour tour, two dollars per fifteen-hour tour.
47. *The Public Employee*, Vol. 35 (April 1970), p. 3.
48. BNA, *Government Employee Relations Report*, No. 358 (July 20, 1970), p. B-11.

Conclusion

Pay and benefits in local governments have advanced impressively. Whether unions can be credited with accelerating wage increases in local governments is to be investigated at length in another study in this series. Cities and counties have had difficulty in financing increases in pay and benefits, and it would be understandable for them to lag behind the rest of the manpower market. Unions have resisted this, pointing out that employees should not be expected to subsidize their governments.

Yet the changes in the amounts of pay and the amounts and nature of benefits are less important than the changes in procedure and relationships, and to some degree in control. Local government employees before the rise of unionism were passive recipients of, or petitioners or lobbyists for, increased pay and benefits. Now they are contenders for them and, at bargaining times, adversaries of management. As powerful blocs of citizens they compete successfully for public resources. They have participated in management's systems for arranging and evaluating jobs, have made their own analyses of labor markets, and have bargained or lobbied for their objectives. They have gained a share in administration, and legislatures and executives have had to surrender part of their control.

Thus far then, unionism has had a profound effect on personnel policies and processes in local government, and present trends are likely to intensify. The effect on work management and finance—to the extent that they can be separated from personnel administration—is also growing, as the next two chapters show.

CHAPTER FIVE

Effect on Work Management and Working Conditions

Unions are obviously interested in how the daily operations of cities and counties are managed, yet this interest is definitely secondary to their concentration on economic issues and on grievances. Despite the overlapping interests discussed in Chapter 2, work management is clearly in the hands of the elected and appointed executives, with little objection from the unions. It is as true in urban government as in private industry that:

In the daily shop work of job assignments, skill classification, production standards, and maintenance of discipline, union officers show little desire to join in managing and in initiating action; they prefer to retain their freedom to protest management's decisions and to stay out of the cross fire of criticism and avoid the wounding resentments of their own members.

Unions have not pushed massively and inexorably into vital policy areas. They have pushed when they could and when it was in their clear interest to do so, advancing when management was careless or weak and retreating when management aggressively resisted them. When unions do enlarge their powers, it is almost always in those areas where they have long been established: wages, hours, and conditions of employment.[1]

Yet one difference from the private sector has been noted above:

1. Neil W. Chamberlain and James W. Kuhn, *Collective Bargaining* (2nd ed., McGraw-Hill, 1965), p. 92

the relationship is less mature.[2] Both sides are feeling their way and have been reluctant to negotiate on matters of program policy and major questions of management. Despite important exceptions, discussed in this chapter, most work management matters handled in formal negotiations are relatively minor.

It is unusual, then, for unions to have a significant effect on work management in the sense of altering policy or executive leadership. Department heads and their assistants are confronted every day with informal complaints and formal grievances about working conditions and supervision, but they are still running the operations. In some governments their power is formalized and recognized in management rights clauses, as was shown in Chapter 2. But the lack of written statements in other localities does not change the situation there, judging by the comments of both management and union leaders. Most of the urban executives interviewed for this study said that unions had had almost no influence on work assignment and supervision, and most of the union leaders agreed—some even adding that they did not seek such influence. Both sides pointed out that informal consultation takes place frequently and organized discussion less often.[3] However, most significant program management decisions are not negotiated.

Several ways in which unions do influence work management are reviewed in this chapter: their resistance to having government work contracted out; their effect on staffing and workload and on assignments of hours and locations; and their concern with the appropriateness of duties of various jobs. Finally, their very considerable influence on working conditions in a narrower sense is discussed.

Resistance to Contracting

For many decades, governments have hired private commercial and industrial firms to do some of their work, usually on grounds of efficiency, economy, and wise use of available resources. Local governments in the United States are no exception. They have contracted out work that requires the temporary use of expensive

2. See p. 59.
3. See p. 29 for reference to union-management councils.

equipment (in the construction of sewers or bridges), or scarce and costly skills (in designing a data processing system for taxes), or independent objectivity (in determining law enforcement policies), or in other circumstances where it is more logical for the government to "hire it done." Using outside firms for these purposes does not usually create employee relations problems.

Unions become deeply interested, however, when a city or county tries to contract out work that is currently being done by government employees, such as trash removal or cleaning of buildings. Management might take this step because the work can be done more cheaply outside, because it is an alternative to a strike by government employees,[4] or for other administrative or political reasons. Whatever the rationale, employees are threatened, unions are threatened, and they resist.

Such resistance is an old and complex story in private-sector labor relations. "Subcontracting," as it is usually called, raises questions of good faith and consistency in management, of economic advantages and disadvantages, and of effects on employees in the bargaining unit. Many of these problems become difficult issues of bargainability or arbitrability. For example, subcontracting may be an unfair labor practice if it is done for the specific purpose of destroying or weakening a union.[5]

Thus far the "contracting-out" issue is less difficult in the public sector than in the private sector and is more potential than real in most of the cities and counties studied here. Their officials maintain that there is no problem, or that the matter "doesn't come up," or that they have a firm policy against contracting out anything except construction. "We feel safer not doing it," remarked one Binghamton executive. Representatives of two governments, however, said that they had considered contracting out services for reasons that did relate to union activity. After a trash collection strike, New Orleans considered the possibility of hiring private

4. John F. Burton, Jr., and Charles Krider, "The Role and Consequences of Strikes by Public Employees," *Yale Law Journal*, Vol. 79 (January 1970), pp. 425–26.

5. Marvin J. Levine, "Subcontracting—Rights and Restrictions," *Personnel*, Vol. 44 (May–June 1967), p. 48. See also Sumner H. Slichter, James J. Healy, and E. Robert Livernash, *The Impact of Collective Bargaining on Management* (Brookings Institution, 1960), Chap. 10; Margaret K. Chandler, *Management Rights and Union Interests* (McGraw-Hill, 1964); and Walter E. Baer, "Subcontracting—Twilight Zone in the Management Function," *Labor Law Journal*, Vol. 16 (October 1965), pp. 643–47.

firms for this service. The Dade County manager's staff deliberated over the possibility of contracting out data processing, hospital food services, and trash collection. The union saw this as a bargaining ploy; whether it was or not, the matter did not advance beyond the stage of conversation. There was some "reverse English" in the attitude of one Dade County union: the firemen urged that the painting of fire stations be contracted out so that they themselves would not have to do it.

Anti-contracting policies of cities and counties receive extra strength and emphasis when they are included in union agreements. For example, the American Federation of State, County, and Municipal Employees (AFSCME) agreement in Buffalo provides that the city will not contract out work that is currently being done by its employees; the Teamsters' pact with Detroit forbids contracting to reduce the city work force; so do the Multnomah County union contracts. Several of the Milwaukee agreements state that unions will be consulted in advance of any contracting decision and that no employee with civil service status will be laid off as a result.[6] By contrast, AFSCME tried but failed to get an anti-contracting clause included in its agreement with Hartford. That city does have a policy, however, that employees will not be laid off except when funds are unavailable.

With or without such provisions unions bring pressure to retain government work for government employees. The Service Employees International Union (SEIU) in Boston prevented management from contracting out janitorial service for the new city hall, while AFSCME succeeded in getting the city to take over the work of one private garbage collection contractor. In Detroit the latter union protested, in vain this time, the contracting out of a refuse loading operation that required the use of large power shovels. In Los Angeles County the California Association of Professional Employees objected to the use of outside architects in preparing county building plans.

Such largely successful union efforts to prevent or limit the contracting out of urban government functions add an important element to an understanding of the employment transaction. They

6. Such an employee may be transferred without loss of pay, but this is not considered a layoff.

mean that governments have agreed to retain work for employees even though there may be otherwise sound management reasons for having the work done by outsiders. Governments have thus surrendered some of their rights to determine management policies. They are obliged, under these anti-contracting pressures, to do their work in such a way as to protect the jobs of certain groups of citizens.

Workload, Manning, and Program Policy

How much influence do unions have over the amount of work assigned, the number of employees needed to do it, the way in which it is done, and the basic content of program policy? To re-emphasize the general conclusion reached here, the influence of unions on these matters is negligible in most cities and in most programs. Yet the exceptions show the kinds of inroads unions can make into work management.

CASEWORKERS IN NEW YORK

The 1965 New York City "welfare strike" profoundly affected labor relations in that city. Before that time city employee unions had bargained primarily on economic issues. But this four-week stoppage eventually resulted in a landmark settlement that provided for a maximum caseload of sixty for a caseworker in the department of social services. The caseworkers struck twice again in 1967 over a complex of issues. They wanted more pay and promotional opportunities and protection against arbitrariness in transfers; but above all, they wanted more influence in determining social policies. The demands of the Social Service Employees Union (SSEU) included: a 25 percent increase in client budgets, automatic twice yearly clothing grants, and telephone allowances. An agreement was reached on salaries, but more than half of the caseworkers refused to work during the period of more than six weeks while "professional issues" were debated. The entire situation was complicated by the aggressive activities of welfare clients' organizations, with which the employee unions sympathized. The outcome was that none of the SSEU demands on behalf of the welfare recipients was granted.[7]

The union's case for policy involvement was clearly stated by its leader soon afterward in another forum. After detailing the pressures on welfare administrators from higher levels of government, influential community sources, and the media, he said,

> We can understand, therefore, why some administrators, often those administrators whose intelligence, dedication and approach to welfare problems we most admire, are moved to adamantly refuse to bargain with the union on matters of policy, seeking refuge instead, under the umbrella of "managerial prerogative."
>
> We understand it, but we cannot accept it. It's a mistake and a grievous one. There are good reasons for the influence of workers to be extended to the policies and purposes of their employer. It is the simple democratic right of workers to participate in the management of their agency. Their job consumes a third of their day, and a major portion of their lives. This is doubly true in welfare where many of the employees have advanced training and almost all of them exhibit unusual interest in their work and in the agency's clients. Nor will this right militate to the detriment of the agency; rather, the influence of workers can and will be a positive one. If the imagination, intelligence and the unique experience of the welfare worker is drawn upon in the formation of agency policies, the full potentiality of welfare departments will better and more effectively be realized. . . .
>
> We do not seek to run the agency. We have enough trouble running our unions. To negotiate is not to dictate; to discuss is not necessarily to accede. The responsibility to bargain does not carry with it the responsibility to accept our every demand, or any demand. However, this responsibility is not satisfied when one party consistently demands unilateral discretion on a multitude of items and refuses to concede any voice in their determination, inserting artificial theoretical barriers between the negotiators. A pragmatic issue by issue approach will bring far better results for all.[8]

The employees' desire for a more definite voice in welfare policy

---

7. See discussion in Gilbert Y. Steiner, *The State of Welfare* (Brookings Institution, 1971), pp. 302–05.

8. Martin Morgenstern, National Coordinator, National Federation of Social Service Employees, "Public Welfare at the Bargaining Table, an Employees' Viewpoint" (paper presented at American Public Welfare Association Round Table, Washington, D.C., Dec. 8, 1967; processed), p. 16.

determination was not really satisfied, but they did advance the frontiers of union involvement in departmental management. Evidence is found in the 1967 SSEU contract, which built upon the 1965 settlement. The contract retains the sixty-caseload figure[9] (requires the department to pay for overtime in cash whenever a caseload rises above sixty) and includes details on reserve staffing patterns.

A reserve field casework staff shall be established in the Department equal to 10% of the number of field and intake Caseworkers. This reserve staff shall be used first on a priority basis to cover temporarily uncovered caseloads, caseloads of persons on vacation and leave and for handling emergencies to the extent possible. When not so employed, the Department shall retain the right to designate appropriate duties for the reserve staff. Ten percent of the budgeted positions for field Caseworkers and intake Caseworkers shall be added to the approved budget lines to create this reserve.[10]

The same contract says that the department will recommend the establishment of four hundred senior caseworker, eight hundred assistant caseworker, and seventy-five senior homemaker positions.[11] Compared to other contract clauses reviewed in the field research for this book, these workload and staffing provisions represent uniquely deep penetrations into what is usually considered management territory.

The net effect of this agreement was to increase the casework staff, but this trend was halted in 1969, when the department of social services adopted new policies endorsed by the U.S. Department of Health, Education, and Welfare. The department stopped using caseworkers to verify the eligibility of each client and substituted a system under which a client qualifies for his benefits by filing a "declaration" at a social service center. Only 10 percent of the cases are investigated; this work, along with a large part of the

9. Other caseload standards are specified for specialized programs, for example, forty for narcotics cases and forty-five for veterans' cases in the bureau of public assistance; and twenty-five for children in the foster family day care program of the bureau of child welfare.

10. Contract between the City of New York and the Department of Social Services and the Social Service Employees Union, Sept. 21, 1967, Article VII.

11. *Ibid.*, Article V.

caseworkers' "bookkeeping" duties, is done by clerical employees.[12] Caseworkers do not check eligibility for payments but provide direct social service to those clients who need it. Although this new plan was strongly opposed by the SSEU and by AFSCME Local 371 (social service supervisors) and Local 1,549 (city-wide clerical workers), management persisted in putting it into effect. However, the city formally agreed to a variety of concessions and safeguards, including: "workload salary adjustment" payments to compensate caseworkers for increased loads; no layoffs or loss of pay, benefits, or promotional opportunities for employees with permanent civil service status; limitations on management's freedom to transfer employees; and establishment of a joint union-management reorganization and workload committee to decide transitional problems during the reorganization. The unions agreed to the abolition of the relatively new senior caseworker title and the downgrading of employees who were serving under that title on a provisional basis. As the new plan was put into effect, management claimed a reduction of 2,200 caseworker jobs and savings of about $17.6 million a year.[13]

OTHER EXAMPLES OF WORKLOAD ISSUES

Social service workers in San Francisco tried in a mild sort of way to emulate those in New York City. They dumped on their supervisors' desks files on any cases in excess of sixty per worker, but desisted when a memorandum from the department head threatened disciplinary action. SSEU also worries about policy. Its members objected to what they considered their department's slow pace in hiring underprivileged citizens in the "new careers" program and its tendency to assign only menial duties to them.

Also in San Francisco, probation officers struck in March 1969 to protest case overloads. They left their jobs after one employee had been suspended for five days for refusing to accept a case in addition to those already assigned to him. Two months later juvenile probation officers walked out when the board of supervisors decided to cut the number of new officers hired from the mayor's

12. Bureau of National Affairs, *Government Employee Relations Report*, No. 281 (Jan. 27, 1969), p. B-3.
13. Peter Kihss, *New York Times*, Feb. 9, 1970.

proposed twenty-four to thirteen. They returned to work when the board approved nine more jobs after learning that the necessary funds would be provided by the state government. Los Angeles County probation officers also threatened to strike over their caseload, but the issue was settled when the county provided additional staff. And to cite one more example from another kind of work and another part of the country, workload standards for book truck drivers and bindery workers in the Milwaukee city library were changed after discussions with the union.

MANNING PROBLEMS

Workload and manning questions cannot really be separated, as is clear from the social worker and probation officer examples discussed above, but unions may emphasize one aspect rather than the other. The number of employees on the job is a prime consideration in some agreements and negotiations. In demanding more employees on the job, unions sometimes claim that this is necessary for safety reasons; sometimes they simply say that more people are needed to do the work.

How Many Firemen? As one example, the following clause from Dade County's agreement with the International Association of Fire Fighters (IAFF) is justified by the union entirely on the basis of employee safety.

Minimum Manning: The County Manager agrees to recommend sufficient combat personnel to provide the following combat equipment manning:

Pumpers—One qualified operator and two combat personnel.

Aerial-Ladder Units—One qualified operator and two additional combat personnel.

Tankers—One qualified operator.[14]

The city management, although agreeing with these proposed levels, encountered budgetary problems in staffing the department to achieve them.

Elsewhere the firemen's unions and the New York City government negotiated for about a year over manning and workload

14. "Firefighters Collective Bargaining" (memorandum from County Manager to Mayor and Members of Board of County Commissioners, Dade County, Florida, May 28, 1968), Provision 9.

problems. The unions initially contended that their workloads were improperly high and demanded that 2,500 officers and firemen be added to the force. The city maintained that manning the department was a managerial prerogative and therefore not subject to bargaining. The city was also seeking more flexibility in assigning fire fighting units to high-risk hours and areas. The unions threatened "job action"—refusal to perform nonfirefighting duties—but this was averted when the city agreed to add 500 firemen and officers and to submit the question of the negotiability of the workload issue to the tripartite board of collective bargaining. Without ruling specifically on the fire department issue, the board decided that any management determination having a "practical impact" on the working conditions of employees may ultimately become the subject of collective bargaining if the city does not "act expeditiously" to relieve the impact.[15] Finally the unions and the city agreed that within a year (from September 1969) 750 firemen and 90 officers would be added "to provide eight new full-time companies and ten tactical units—seven-man volunteer teams that would work in the high-alarm hours from 3 p.m. to 1 a.m."[16]

Two-man Patrol Cars and Other Safety Issues. Whether a police patrol car should be manned by one or two officers is a subject of controversy in urban governments. The police unions insist that two men are required at all times for effective law enforcement and for the safety of the men. Management maintains—successfully in most localities—that this decision is a management prerogative and that one man is enough in the safer neighborhoods during the safer times of day. In New York City, however, the issue was formally contested and went to arbitration. The city won the decision, but union pressures were strong enough to prevent its implementation—even though the city bought some three hundred vehicles designed for one-man use.

Safety in the inner city affects more than the police. Staffing increases were urged upon the New York City Youth Board by its union so that recreation leaders would not have to work alone in hazardous areas. The same issue came up in Detroit for other occupations. Unions there demanded that health inspectors, weights

15. New York City Board of Collective Bargaining, Decision No. B-9-68, Nov. 12, 1968. See also the discussion of management rights in Chap. 2 above.

16. Maurice Carroll, *New York Times*, Sept. 18, 1969.

and measures inspectors, and dog catchers work in two-man teams for safety. The decisions still remained in the hands of management in 1971; more men are assigned if they are available. Safety in another sense (guarding against accidents) was the reason for the union's success in Detroit in insisting that a foreman always be assigned to treetopping crews in the parks.

Safety is also the heading under which the following manning requirement appears in the New York sanitationmen's contract:

> Each escalator and compactor truck employed in the collection of household refuse shall be manned by a crew consisting of three Sanitationmen who shall be responsible for the driving and loading. Any exception can be made only after discussion with the Union.[17]

Obviously such a requirement helps minimize injuries (for example, two men would lift a heavy can), but it also means more men to get the work done (they can go home when they finish their routes) and more union members.

Other New York Examples. Years ago union concern for having enough men assigned to a task resulted in a standard practice in the New York department of public works of putting five-man crews on relatively small highway and sewer repair jobs: a foreman, a motor vehicle operator, and three laborers. Management tried to eliminate the motor vehicle operator and have one of the laborers drive. They were unsuccessful at first, but the proposal was adopted later when the department was reorganized. More recently safety, beauty, and quality of service were all emphasized in a strong attack by an AFSCME publication on reduced maintenance staffing by the New York department of parks.[18]

Technological Change. The use of labor-saving equipment, long a labor issue in private industry,[19] has drawn little attention as yet in local governments. An article in *Nation's Cities* in 1970, for example, reported on the results of a trial study of a new one-man trash collection truck. The piece did acknowledge the need for upgrading personnel to perform the work and mentions fatigue

17. Contract Between the Uniformed Sanitationmen's Association and the Department of Sanitation of the City of New York (effective June 7, 1967) (Uniformed Sanitationmen's Association, 1967), pp. 20–21.

18. Martin Tolchin, *New York Times,* March 20, 1970.

19. For example, see Paul T. Hartman, *Collective Bargaining and Productivity: The Longshore Mechanization Agreement* (University of California Press, 1969).

and safety considerations. Nothing was said, however, about how such a change would be perceived by organized labor—or what difficulties in getting it adopted might be created by the union.[20]

The field research in Detroit revealed a case where union interest was expressed. Management proposed increasing the productivity of garbage collection trips by using a rig known as a "mother-loader," a garbage truck towing a trailer. The employees took one look at it, changed its name, and started for home. Management soon dropped the idea because the equipment had technical, as well as labor-relations, drawbacks. Subsequently the same union (the Teamsters) obtained agreement from the city that proposals for new equipment would be referred to the civil service commission to determine what their effect would be on job classifications. Comparable trouble was avoided in Milwaukee, when a water filtration plant became an automatic operation. The AFSCME agreement provided that the filtration operators whose jobs were affected would be reassigned.

In addition to manning problems that came up formally and publicly, there were many informal discussions, for example, when the Hartford park workers questioned the size of crews and the Los Angeles County nurses urged an improvement in the nurse-patient ratio. In general, however, the unions, despite their obvious concern, are concentrating on other issues.

The Manning Issue in General. Despite the unions' general inactivity in this area, the examples presented, particularly the New York fire and police cases, point to future collisions in other governments between the desire of unions to maintain or increase the number of jobs and the determination of government officials to make their own decisions about the numbers of employees needed to perform services. Such collisions will be few in the near future because of the unions' preoccupation with other objectives and because of the strength of management rights clauses, which reserve manning decisions to the governments. Controversies will also be headed off or reduced in intensity if management officials consult unions on manning problems before taking action and if both the agreements and the civil service rules contain realistic and humane measures to protect employees' job security, such as reassignment provisions and layoff formulas based on seniority.

20. "One-Man Collection Crews Get a Boost," *Nation's Cities,* Vol. 8 (March 1970), pp. 26–28.

Nevertheless, it will be surprising if mature, aggressive unions in many cities do not question or contest the effects of management's decisions about numbers of employees. This expectation follows from the increasingly bilateral nature of the employment relationship and the progressive weakening of management rights in the private sector.[21] Chief executives and legislative bodies should and will decide initially how many employees shall be used on which functions. Lower supervisory officials will decide how many shall be used on specific tasks. Management has the constitutional duty to take these initiatives. Officials have been elected or appointed to carry out the will of the voters in these ways. Yet to the extent that organized employees (who are also voters and pressure groups themselves) can show that manning decisions affect the difficulty and safety of their work, management will be compelled to treat the *impacts* of such decisions as subjects for bargaining or arbitration.

Work Assignments—When and Where?

Unions have penetrated farther—but still not very far—into the area of management's right to decide when and where employees will work. Management as a general rule decides who will work overtime, who will work what shifts, and who will be assigned to what location. Yet this authority is also being increasingly weakened under union pressures.

ASSIGNING OVERTIME WORK

Ordering employees to work overtime has long been treated as a basic management "right" in the public service. Like other management "rights," however, it is part of the employment transaction and endures only as long as it is accepted. The right is more important in principle than in practice for two reasons. First, union members usually want to work overtime to earn extra pay; thus, the problem is who shall be granted the benefit of overtime work rather than who shall be forced to work against his will. Second, in a genuine public emergency requiring overtime, employees have generally cooperated. Still the principle has been violated.

21. See the discussion of management rights in Chap. 2, pp. 21-25.

Management officials in Hartford, New Castle County, and Wilmington have agreed that they will not assign employees to overtime work without their consent.[22] A lesser modification has occurred in Buffalo, where employees can be required to work overtime without their consent only in emergencies, and in Multnomah County and Philadelphia, only when the public health and safety require it.

Determining how overtime is assigned is usually treated as a management prerogative. When the matter is mentioned in union agreements,[23] it is usually assumed that employees want overtime, and the agreements direct that it be distributed equally among employees of the same class in the organization concerned. New Castle County and Wilmington are exceptions because they use seniority as a criterion. One New Castle County official said that the county had tried rotating overtime among employees at the union's request but, when this did not work well, changed to a seniority basis.

SHIFT ASSIGNMENTS

Management's right to assign employees to day or night shifts is increasingly weakened by union agreements specifying that assignments will be made according to seniority among those desiring certain shifts. (Some employees avoid late shifts; others want them because a differential is usually paid.) Examples are the Teamsters and hospital unions' pacts in Detroit, the Sanitationmen's in New York, and AFSCME's in five smaller governments.

Unions can succeed in getting shift assignment clauses put into agreements to solve local problems. For example, to insure fair coverage of undesirable shifts, the union at San Francisco's Laguna Honda Hospital negotiated the following:

Subject to the availability of personnel the Hospital agrees that in staffing shifts personnel will be reasonably distributed.[24]

22. Overtime can be required of policemen and firemen in Hartford.

23. A majority of the agreements in the nineteen governments studied do not mention it.

24. "Interim Memorandum of Understanding," written agreement between Laguna Honda Hospital and Hospital and Institutional Workers Local 250, AFL-CIO, April 29, 1969, p. 14.

Another section of the same agreement reads:

As a reduction of split shift permanent positions occur [sic] or as permanent straight shift positions are vacated, employees on split shifts in order of seniority will be given the choice of assignment to permanent straight shift positions.[25]

And the Dade County firemen, in order to stabilize their days off, won this:

The County Manager shall direct the Fire Chief to make every possible effort to minimize the transfer of personnel between shifts and duty assignments which would result in changes in the number of working hours in an average three-week period.[26]

Park concession workers in the same county were not so successful. Working a six-day, forty-hour week scheduled each day to serve peak park loads, they urged the department director to let them work their forty hours in five days but were refused.

There was a prolonged conflict between union and management in the 1969 "fourth platoon" controversy in New York City. The mayor and the police commissioner sought repeal of a fifty-eight year old state law that established three—and only three—eight-hour patrol shifts a day for city policemen—midnight to 8 a.m., 8 a.m. to 4 p.m., and 4 p.m. to midnight. The city wanted to create a fourth platoon to patrol during the high-crime hours—6 p.m. to 2 a.m. The proposal was strongly resisted by the Patrolmen's Benevolent Association, which was uninhibited by the logic of the suggestion and by the presumably damaging disclosures that some on-duty policemen slept in the small hours.

After the repeal was enacted, the union sued to void it, contending that the question of an additional shift had been considered in collective bargaining and discarded and that the new law violated a management-union contract. The court rejected the suit.

The basic issue was of course control of police assignments. In a full-page newspaper ad, the union declared that the bill

would give Lindsay the uncontrolled right to play field marshal with New York's law enforcement officers! Vesting of such arbitrary power when no emergency exists is unthinkable! . . .

The purpose of the Three-Platoon Law was to insure that police officers would be given the security of regular tours of duty according to a pre-determined schedule, and to guarantee that at least one-third of their working time be scheduled during normal daylight hours except in emergencies. This assurance of regularity is essential if patrolmen and their families are to adjust to the unnatural demands of around-the-clock service. Even under the mild limitations of the present law, a patrolman's customary working hours change every week.[27]

The union proposed instead special volunteer forces during high-crime hours. However, management responded that the volunteer system would not meet public safety needs and would be vulnerable to arbitrary stoppages through "job action" by the PBA. The fourth platoon was started on a voluntary basis, even though mangement had won legal power to order it—a clear indication of union strength. In September 1969 it was in effect in thirty-six of the city's seventy-nine precincts.[28]

WORK LOCATIONS

In several cities there has been a weakening of management's authority to assign employees to other locations, or to other jobs in the same class and location. Union agreements in Buffalo, Detroit, Hartford, and Multnomah County provide that such assignments are to be allotted on the basis of seniority among those who wish to make a change. Examples were also found in the latter three governments of assignment of less desirable work to employees with less seniority.

The New York social service unions, whose trailbreaking work has already been discussed, bargained for an elaborate and rigorous system of controls on transfers in connection with their staff reduction. The following priorities were specified:

1. Volunteers in order of seniority.
2. Non-volunteers by inverse order of seniority.
3. Employees under extended probation or special evaluatory supervision who have received written notice of such status.
4. Travel hardship cases [defined as travel time of 55 minutes or more for city residents and of 1¼ hours or more for noncity residents].
5. Employees with less than six months of service in a title.
6. Employees who have been transferred within the past twelve months.
7. Medical and personal hardship cases.[29]

27. *New York Times,* March 22, 1969.
28. Maurice Carroll, *New York Times,* Sept. 12, 1969.
29. "Interim Understanding," submitted by negotiating representatives of the City

Other paragraphs develop the requirements in more detail.

Trash collection routes, although under management control, probably cause more union–management discussion than any other work-location and workload questions in urban governments. For one thing the trash collectors are likely to be well organized and aggressive. Second, the planning of routes is a difficult management problem involving distance, type of area, traffic problems, types of trash, and other variables. Third, the men are generally allowed to go home when they finish their routes and hence prefer the routes that are nearest their homes. Earnest discussion of routes was reported, for example, in Dade County, Dayton, and New Orleans. Routes in Detroit cannot be changed without two weeks' notice to, and a special conference with, the union, and in New York the union has virtually complete veto power.

Whose Work?

In the discussion of classification (Chapter 4) the unions' interest in job duties and their vigilance in limiting actual work performance to those duties were emphasized. It was also noted (in Chapter 3) that arguments about appropriate work assignments may end in formal grievances. Management and unions in Milwaukee have tried to limit such problems by stating in their agreements that incidental job duties are not always specified.

In keeping an eye on out-of-title work, unions look up, down, and sideways. They want their members to get higher pay if they are temporarily assigned to higher-rated jobs; they do not want their members to work beneath their skills; and they are sensitive to potential problems of labor jurisdiction. All this limits management's discretion in achieving short-term on-the-job efficiency by requiring employees to do "related work."[30] Management usually prevails, but, as was pointed out earlier, management is much more careful than it used to be.

Dade County firemen successfully objected to doing major repair work on hydrants but agreed to minor maintenance work—

---

of New York and District Council 37, Locals 371 and 1549 of AFSCME, AFL-CIO, and the Social Service Employees Union (1969; processed), p. 2.

30. For decades government job descriptions have included some such phrase as "performs related work as required." Union pressures are making these words extinct.

checking and painting. Firemen in Cincinnati, on the other hand, do no maintenance at all. Lifeguards in Dade County complained in vain about doing maintenance chores in bad weather.

Union pressures in Buffalo and New York City stopped policemen from operating tow trucks. In New York this resulted from an arbitrator's decision in a case initiated by the motor vehicle operators' union. Yet police unions in Boston and San Francisco prevented other employees—police cadets and civilian parking patrolmen, respectively—from directing traffic.[31]

It is not unusual for efficiency experts, civic groups, and out-of-office politicians to urge that more civilians be employed to do office work in police departments, thus releasing uniformed personnel for street duty. Several candidates promoted this in the 1969 New York mayoral campaign. On the whole the police have successfully resisted such proposals, claiming that the jobs are needed for men whose physical condition limits them to light duty and that police training is needed to do the work with adequate understanding. Such pressure was unsuccessful in Boston, however, and police desk work was assigned to civilians.

Other examples: The Teamsters in Detroit insisted that a materials technician not be permitted to drive a soil boring rig because this is drivers' work. Basin machine operators in New York, although willing to remove manhole covers, draw the line at stone slabs.

In another area, subprofessional work in hospitals seems to be passed down to lower echelons. Registered nurses pass work down to licensed practical nurses (LPNs), and they in turn pass work to orderlies, food service personnel, and porters. Instances were encountered of LPNs refusing to wash bedsteads and of orderlies refusing to deliver meals.

Such literal dedication to the job description is both good and bad for administration. Management is more orderly, and better use is made of the skills of employees, but operations become more rigid and sometimes slower than they would be if prescribed duties were less meticulously followed. Common sense in management suggests that a truck driver might help carry a piece of furniture to his truck instead of reading a magazine, or that a practical

---

31. The San Francisco traffic code was later amended to permit persons other than police officers to direct traffic in certain situations.

nurse might deliver a meal before it cools off. Yet excessive assignments of improper duties are an imposition on employees and a sign of sloppy administration. If both management and labor try to get the job done and to communicate well with one another, they can keep down the amount of quibbling over duty assignments.

Working Conditions

The term "working conditions" is sometimes defined broadly enough to include the matters discussed thus far in this chapter, but the definition can be narrowed to more immediate physical circumstances at the job, such as safety equipment, clothing, and tools. It is not easy to determine what effect unions have had on these conditions. Both management and unions have a stake in effective working arrangements, and both have a genuine interest in the well-being of employees. Unions may speed up certain improvements by exerting pressure on management, or they may actually delay them by forcing management to spend the necessary funds on something else.

Some management officials, notably in Binghamton, Cincinnati, New Castle County, and Philadelphia, said that unions had had little impact on working conditions. Yet in all of these localities, examples of improvements made under union pressure were found. In fact a Cincinnati union agreement says that management cannot change working conditions without consulting the union. A few agreements in other cities specify that employees may appeal unsatisfactory working conditions under the grievance procedure.

A bewildering variety of detailed conditions can be and are covered in union–management negotiations, but by far the most numerous items of concern relate to either safety or clothing.

SAFETY

Work safety is normally emphasized in agreements as a responsibility of both parties. This is sometimes buttressed by a joint union–management safety committee, which is required by contract in Binghamton, Boston, Hartford, and Milwaukee. Yet when the unions in Detroit asked for such a committee, management refused. Said a key city official, "We don't want men putting red flags on equipment; a little knowledge is a dangerous thing." He added, however, that rapid action is taken to solve cases when employees are reluctant to operate what they think is unsafe equipment.

Safety discussions often emphasize protective devices or measures. For example, red flags were put on Cincinnati street cleaners' carts at the suggestion of the union; the SEIU in San Francisco objected to having female hospital orderlies lift patients; and Dade County supplied safety shoes to garbage men and pavement workers at union urging. In New York a union persuaded the Department of Markets to close an unsafe building that housed inspectors' offices. Unsafe trucks were targets for union protests in many cities and led to a two-day strike in New Orleans.[32] Union pressure in Wilmington forced the city to equip trash trucks with first-aid kits—which unfortunately disappeared soon thereafter.

In addition to maintaining their interest in safety in this traditional industrial sense, unions are becoming more concerned about the physical safety of their members who work in civil disorders. The Hartford, Milwaukee, and New York police have all demanded—and received—hard hats. So have the San Francisco police, who also wanted something they did not get—the chemical mace. Milwaukee policemen were given safety glasses, corrective if necessary, and firemen in several cities received shields on their trucks to protect them from thrown missiles. Although fire fighters in Detroit asked for the right to carry weapons, they were turned down.

Disease prevention has also become a labor relations matter. An SEIU local objected strenuously to the practice in a Los Angeles county hospital of using the same truck ramp both for removing garbage and for delivering fresh food. Management first denied the existence of the problem and then eliminated it. In Detroit the Teamsters insisted that maggoty garbage trucks be hosed down; health inspectors bargained for annual X-rays, blood tests, and urinalyses; and dog pound workers won a variety of health safeguards. New York was threatened with an enormous traffic tie-up

32. Bureau of National Affairs, *Government Employee Relations Report*, No. 379 (Dec. 14, 1970), p. B-14.

on Thanksgiving Day 1969, when toll collectors of the Triborough Bridge and Tunnel Authority threatened to strike over being subjected to so much air pollution. They stayed on the job after assurances that they would receive health examinations and that levels of contamination at their duty locations would be measured professionally. They struck for four days over the same issue nine months later but went back to work when the Authority agreed to install high-speed fans.

CLOTHING

Management's obligation to provide or pay for garments can be regarded as a working condition, but it also can be treated as an economic issue. Work clothing is not difficult to price, and if management does not pay for it, employees must. In any case, clothing or clothing allowances are more and more being regarded as a management responsibility, and union pressures are accelerating the trend. While sometimes "clothing" provisions in union contracts relate to health and safety, such as gloves and rain gear for trash collectors, in many instances no reference is made to this subject. It was found that, as a general practice, management pays for any special garments that employees are *required* to wear on the job.

Naturally, prices differ from one city to another, and costs are going up. Police plain clothesmen receive a clothing allowance of $2 a week in Hartford, $260 a year in Dade County. Boston firemen get a $100 annual allowance for uniforms, while those in Milwaukee get $135. Some of the indications of escalation disclosed in the field research for this study include a 5 percent increase in the uniform allowance given to Binghamton police and an increase from $40 to $100 annually for hospital nurses in Detroit; yet Cincinnati firemen were denied a raise from $65 to $150. And on the question of clothing, Detroit health inspectors bargained for, and won, the right to wear sport shirts while working.

OTHER CONDITIONS

Rest periods and wash-up times are also frequent questions for negotiation. Coffee breaks are generally observed—usually fifteen minutes each half shift, sometimes fifteen minutes each day. They are not mentioned in union contracts in Cincinnati, Dade County, Dayton, and Hartford but nevertheless are granted. Many agreements also provide for fifteen minutes wash-up time before lunch and before the end of the shift. One Detroit department head, reflecting on the time lost for these purposes, grumpily observed that a person can wash his hands in one minute.

Other privileges and conditions are bargained, discussed, or provided by management, but patterns of practice are not clear. Washrooms, locker rooms, and lunchrooms are important to employees. The following excerpt from the New York sanitationmen's agreement sets forth objectives in unusual detail:

1. Each employee shall have his own individual locker.
2. The Department shall make every effort to provide the following equipment, maintained at all times in good working order and in proper quantity; clean lavatory facilities; shower and wash basin facilities with hot and cold running water; heating facilities; proper ventilation; proper lighting and ample supplies of soap, other cleansers, paper towels, paper tissue and other clean-up materials.[33]

Meal allowances are specified in some agreements for occasions when employees must work well beyond their usual hours. Dayton and Hartford provide $1.50 per meal; Wilmington, $1.75; and New Castle County, $2.00.

Mileage allowances for employees using their own automobiles on official business are also bargained or argued about in a few of these governments. Union activity in Multnomah County brought about a standardization of differing allowances, and city inspectors in Detroit won a case against the city's reimbursement formula.

By far the most exhaustive catalogue of required working conditions was achieved by the SSEU in New York, which was a trailbreaker on other questions, as has been noted above. The union's contract contains unusually detailed provisions on working time and free time, including: travel time to get pay checks; grace periods for handicapped employees at the beginning and end of shifts; grace periods for delays due to inadequate elevator service; dismissal at 3 p.m. if the temperature reaches 92 degrees F.; dismissal at noon if the temperature falls below 50 degrees outside and 68

33. Contract Between the Uniformed Sanitationmen's Association and the Department of Sanitation of the City of New York (effective June 7, 1967), p. 19.

degrees inside; or if it falls below those levels after 12 noon, dismissal within an hour.[34] Further on (and it seems sad that this has to be specified), the contract assures the employee of a place to sit down, water to drink, a place to hang his coat, and—obviously essential in view of the preceding requirements—a thermometer. This portion of the contract is reproduced in Appendix C.

Conclusion

Management is still in the saddle, but the straps are loosening. Unions do not claim the right to determine policy or to plan how operations will be managed. They recognize that management has those rights as part of the employment transaction. However, they do assert the right to discuss, and if necessary to object to, management actions that affect employees' work. Such discussions and objections have covered a wide range, from a minor grievance to an issue of the magnitude of the "fourth platoon" question (see pages 103–04, above) in the New York police department.

Unions have been effective in persuading urban governments not to contract out work that public employees can do and in obtaining desired working conditions in a narrow sense: coffee breaks, clothing allowances, safety equipment. They have not been as successful in assuring members that assignments to desirable shifts and locations are made on a seniority basis; and, with scattered exceptions, they have had even less success in their efforts to control or adjust workloads and manning.

---

34. Contract between the City of New York and the Department of Social Services, and the Social Service Employees Union, Sept. 21, 1967, Article VIII.

CHAPTER SIX

Effect on Budget and Finance

Local government employee unions have added new stresses to the already difficult financial situation of these governments but have not basically altered the budget and finance processes. Department heads still prepare preliminary estimates of expenditures. Budget and finance officers organize and adjust the requests of department heads and estimate available revenues. Chief executives make "final" decisions on the budget to be submitted to the legislative body, and the latter holds hearings, approves the budget, and sets tax rates. All this is familiar. What the unions have done is to assume a greatly strengthened and highly visible role in decisions that ultimately have a major impact on the size of the budget. Their political and emotional effect is heightened by the fact that the larger local governments are generally either in or approaching a condition of financial crisis.

Fiscal plight has become a way of municipal life the country over. One would be hard put to identify a city—or for that matter a state, a school district, or a county—that today can see its way clear to a balanced budget for just two or three years ahead, to a budget balanced at an adequate level.[1]

The Fiscal Problem of Local Governments

The nature of this crisis is explained and documented in the extensive literature on the subject, but the main elements of the problem can be summarized as follows.[2] Essentially, costs are rising at a more rapid rate than are revenues. In the case of New York, "Operating costs keep expanding at the rate of about 15 percent a year, while revenues have been growing at the rate of only 5 percent a year."[3] The typical central city is suffering from rapidly escalating expenditures for education, health, public safety, and (to the extent that it is a function of local government) welfare. Part of the increase is sheer inflation, but much of it is rooted in sociological and demographic causes. Upper- and middle-class citizens move to the suburbs, fleeing from—but at the same time contributing to—the deterioration of the central city and leaving behind the higher-cost and lower-paying citizens.

With a few exceptions among the large cities, most of the revenue that local governments can raise comes from property taxes.[4] Property tax revenues increase, but not at a rate that keeps pace with the economy and not nearly enough to keep up with local government expenditures. Tax rates have been raised somewhat, but the increases are restricted both because of limits set in state laws and because of fears that taxpayers will revolt politically or will move out. Local government finance officers would like to impose taxes that are more "elastic" (that is, more responsive to economic changes), such as local sales and income taxes. Yet local po-

1. L. L. Ecker-Racz, "New Directions in Intergovernmental Fiscal Relations," *Minnesota Municipalities* (September 1969), pp. 278 ff.

2. See section 9 of the Bibliography.

3. Richard Phalon, *New York Times*, Oct. 6, 1968.

4. Property taxes comprised 86 percent of all local government taxes in 1967–68 and 66 percent of all general revenue from local government sources. Advisory Commission on Intergovernmental Relations, *State and Local Finances: Significant Features, 1967 to 1970* (ACIR, 1969), p. 31.

litical pressures or the need to obtain authority from reluctant state legislatures prevents these levies from going high enough really to solve the problem. Another potential remedy is suggested when local governments solicit aid money—either for general purposes or for particular programs—from their state capitals. Unfortunately, however, most states have their own financial problems, and their legislatures (which are more responsive to rural and suburban areas) are not disposed to help the cities much if it would mean putting the state more deeply in debt.

Despite this gloomy picture, local governments could improve the administration of their property taxes with the aid of state-imposed standards and state-donated technical assistance. A better tax balance could be achieved among neighboring communities and more equal burdens among taxpayers. The revenue potentials of escalating land values could be more fully realized.[5]

Ambitious proposals have also been made to permit the local governments to share the superior fiscal resources of higher levels of government. The Advisory Commission on Intergovernmental Relations has urged that local governments be relieved of the financial burdens of welfare and education, with the federal government assuming all of the former and state governments assuming the latter. There is also wide support for plans to share the federal government's income with states and cities. Says one proponent, "There is no hope for the states and local governments, whatever they do on their own initiative, unless the federal government cuts them in on its superior tax resources."[6] Revenue sharing was endorsed by President Nixon in 1969, 1970, and 1971.[7] Yet all of these proposals face formidable political and financial obstacles, and be-

5. See Dick Netzer, "The Budget: Trends and Prospects," in Lyle C. Fitch and Annmarie Hauck Walsh (eds.), *Agenda for a City: Issues Confronting New York* (Sage Publications, 1970), pp. 677–89.

6. Joseph A. Pechman, "The Rich, the Poor, and the Taxes They Pay," *The Public Interest* (Fall 1969), p. 35. See also Harvey S. Perloff and Richard P. Nathan (eds.), *Revenue Sharing and the City* (Johns Hopkins Press, 1968).

7. "The President's Address to the Nation on Domestic Programs," Aug. 8, 1969. For text, see *Weekly Compilation of Presidential Documents,* Vol. 5 (Aug. 11, 1969), pp. 1103–12. See also Michael E. Levy, "Sharing Federal Revenue with the States: A Comparison of the ACIR and Nixon Proposals," *The Conference Board Record,* Vol. 7 (April 1970), pp. 3–12; Warren Weaver, Jr., "Revenue-Sharing Revived by Nixon," *New York Times,* Aug. 20, 1970; and "The State of the Union," The President's Message Delivered before a Joint Session of Congress, January 22, 1971, published in *Weekly Compilation of Presidential Documents,* Vol. 7 (Jan. 25, 1971), pp. 89–97.

leaguered city finance officers cannot look to them for early or significant relief.

Putting the Budget Together

Before looking at the effect of union pressures on the size of budgets and on financing measures a review should be made of their impact on budget preparation. This tends to be a belated impact, usually near the end of the decision-making process.

In these nineteen localities, as in most fair-sized local governments, budget preparation begins about six months before the start of the new fiscal year when the budget office sends to the various department heads instructions on the format and schedule to be followed in preparing estimates. Departments may or may not be told how rigorously to economize or what programs to emphasize as they look ahead. Generally using the current budget figures as a base, department heads make their estimates, often in consultation with a member of the budget staff. Where it is feasible they use workload figures, past and estimated, to back up their calculations—numbers of fires, miles of streets, cubic yards of rubbish. The department heads do not consult unions at this time and are influenced by union pressures only to the extent that previous union-sponsored changes in work rules or pay provisions have changed the expense outlook. Meanwhile the budget office (or the finance staff if it is a separate organization) is estimating expected revenues. Then both revenue and expenditure sheets go to the chief executive, who, aided by the budget and finance staff, must trim the expense estimates, or plan to seek extra revenues, or both, in order to balance his budget before it goes to the legislative body.[8]

In the days before unions acquired collective bargaining rights, this budget process readily accommodated changes in pay and benefits. Modifications were proposed by the personnel office or civil service commission, approved by the budget office and chief executive, and ultimately enacted by the legislative body. They were

8. For a concise, sophisticated summary of local government budgeting, see John P. Crecine, "A Computer Simulation Model of Municipal Budgeting," *Management Science*, Vol. 13 (July 1967), pp. 786–815.

kept within anticipated financial resources and were usually timed to begin at the start of the next fiscal year. In the present era of collective bargaining, even though most of the budget process is unrelated to union activities, the schedule has become less controllable for three reasons. First, the bargaining process is time-consuming. Second, unions may adopt a strategy that calls for bargaining to reach a climax at the time the legislative body is considering the budget. Third, the results of bargaining may require new financing measures involving further legislation locally, or a referendum, or action by the state legislature. However, in situations where there is a multi-year union agreement, without pay reopener provisions, such problems are spaced out and therefore less troublesome.

Cities in New York State (including, among those studied, Binghamton and Buffalo but not New York City) are expected to be kept on schedule by the Taylor Law, which provides that negotiations, including mediation and fact finding, must be concluded sixteen days before the budget is submitted to the local legislative body.[9] Despite the law, Buffalo ran late in 1968. That city's charter requires the mayor to submit the budget to the council by May 1 for adoption by June 1. However, when the 1968 union negotiations (the first under the law) had not been completed by June 1, the city had to include a lump-sum "salary adjustment fund" in the budget to cover the estimated costs of the union settlements.

Several of the cities and counties in other states try to complete bargaining before the legislative body starts work on the budget. Hartford has been successful thus far in concluding negotiations well before the budget is closed, even though state law permits bargaining to run on beyond that time. The city aims to finish bargaining by January 1 and to pass the budget in February; the fiscal year begins April 1. Still another method was found in Detroit, where pay discussions are part of the budget process and separate from union negotiations on other matters. Pay settlements there are not included in agreements, but are recommended by the mayor to the common council along with the budget.

9. New York, Public Employees' Fair Employment Act of 1967, sec. 209, as amended, March 4, 1969. Section 212 of the law exempts New York City from this requirement.

Two governments, Dade County and Philadelphia, bargain while the legislative body has the budget under review but before it completes action.

In a still later category are cities and counties where bargaining continues even after the budget is adopted. This means that if the budget does not contain enough funds to finance the agreement, additional revenues must be obtained. Boston, Dayton, New Castle County, and New York have all been in the position of concluding agreements after the budget has been decided. Boston lacks a fixed schedule for both budget submissions and bargaining. Although the fiscal year there begins in January, departmental estimates trickle in until April, when a supplementary budget request based on bargaining settlements is submitted to the city council. The tax rate is set the following July. New York City's scores of agreements are concluded at different times of the year (usually January or July) and vary in their duration; hence it is virtually impossible to budget realistically for bargaining settlements. Budgeting and bargaining have become two very separate operations.

Turning to the four governments that do not have general collective bargaining, in Los Angeles County, New Orleans, and San Francisco the personnel authorities recommend salaries and benefits for consideration by the legislative bodies before budgets are adopted. St. Louis has found it necessary in the past to consider the salary demands of the unions after the budget is adopted. However, tentative agreement has now been reached between the city and four unions to conduct annual negotiating sessions *before* the budget is drafted.[10]

Reconciling the budget schedule with the bargaining schedule is an annual problem where the agreements are for one year only.[11] Elsewhere these coordination problems have to be faced only in the years when agreements are up for renewal.

10. Bureau of National Affairs, *Government Employee Relations Report,* No. 358 (July 20, 1970), p. B-13.
11. One-year agreements are made in Binghamton, Dade County, Detroit, Multnomah County, and Tacoma. Bargaining occurs every three years in Hartford and every two years in Buffalo, New Castle County, and New York City (where agreements overlap, as was noted above). There is a mixture of one- and two-year agreements in Milwaukee and Dayton. Philadelphia had a city-wide agreement for two years, followed by one for eighteen months. Wilmington has two-year contracts, but the subjects of wages and fringes can be reopened.

WHAT TIMING IS BEST?

Financial management is obviously more efficient when negotiations are finished before the budget goes to the legislature. Under such circumstances the executive branch has considered the unions' demands along with other spending needs and with estimated revenues, reconciled any problems, and prepared a budget package that is fully ready for legislative action. This is hard to achieve for reasons already stated: slow bargaining, union strategies, and authorization of supplementary financing. The experience of the governments studied here suggests that bargaining results can feasibly go to the legislative body *after* it has begun work on the budget. It is even possible for bargaining to be completed after the budget has been approved by the legislature. In either event the budget process becomes more protracted, less businesslike, and less controllable from a management standpoint. The city council may have to enact supplementary appropriations and new revenue measures after the start of the new fiscal period.

Several of the governments studied have adapted themselves to these difficulties. The problems perhaps would be lessened if elected officials, citizens' groups, and the news media brought pressure for timely conclusion of bargaining. The union members too would like to have their uncertainties ended sooner—but not at the cost of lower settlements. It seems inevitable on the whole that rigid bargaining schedules to meet budget deadlines will be viewed with more nostalgia than respect. Delayed and revised budgets are inconvenient and stressful for executives and staffs and are more difficult for citizens to understand, but they can be expected to continue, and local governments will make the necessary adaptations.

RESERVES FOR SETTLEMENTS

Representatives of all the cities and counties, regardless of their budget schedules, were asked if they budgeted any "cushions" (contingency funds) or if they "hid" any money to pay for union settlements that were higher than they had anticipated. A majority of the governments studied answered in the negative. Buffalo,

Hartford, Milwaukee, and New Castle County all reported that they use contingency funds for this purpose. One other county and three cities, whose identity will not be disclosed, candidly said that they "hid" money in the estimates for various departments. The former method (use of an earmarked fund) is risky. It may become a "sitting duck" for legislators who want to eliminate it or use it for another purpose; or it may become a target for bargaining demands—unions may ask for the total amount and more too. Cincinnati operates under another method, financing settlements out of an "income tax permanent improvement fund," which receives income tax revenues that exceed estimates. The city manager commits part of the fund to capital improvement projects, but it is difficult for the unions to find out how much is uncommitted, thus giving the city some bargaining leeway.

PROGRAM PLANNING AND BUDGETING SYSTEMS

To determine the relationship of unionism to the budget process, officials were asked about the extent to which a planning-programming-budgeting system (PPBS)[12] was used in the city or county concerned. There was found to be some use of PPBS in seven of the nineteen localities,[13] but no attempt was made to connect this to the interest of unions. PPBS generally concentrates on program objectives and activities, and one program may involve several organizational units, several bargaining units, and some unorganized employees. The analytical studies in these localities had no visible effect on the incomes, work methods, or relationships of

12. PPBS is a method for determining government objectives over a period of years and evaluating the effectiveness of existing and proposed programs as a basis for budget formulation. See "A Symposium—Planning-Programming-Budgeting System Reexamined: Development, Analysis, and Criticism," *Public Administration Review*, Vol. 29 (March/April 1969), pp. 111–202 (especially Selma J. Mushkin, "PPB in Cities," pp. 167–78). See also Selma J. Mushkin, "PPBS in City, State, and County: An Overview," in *Innovations in Planning, Programing, and Budgeting in State and Local Governments*, A Compendium of Papers Submitted to the Subcommittee on Economy in Government of the Joint Economic Committee, 91 Cong. 1 sess. (1969), pp. 1–14; Carter F. Bales, *Implementing PPBS in the City of New York*, Special Bulletin 1969C (Municipal Finance Officers Association, October 1969); Edwin Brenman, "Budgeting: How It's Done in the Nation's Largest City," *Public Management*, Vol. 51 (August 1969), pp. 3–5.

13. Boston, Dade County, Dayton, Detroit, Los Angeles County, New York, and Philadelphia.

union members. If PPBS in the future becomes the basis for a significant reallocation of resources among programs, jobs will be affected, and unions will be heard from. The research for this study suggests, however, that this is no more than a possibility. Many years will elapse, and much staff work will have to be done before most local governments develop the analytical capability to put PPBS into effect. If such work can develop reliable indices of work productivity, this will be a useful foundation for collective bargaining as well as for program budgeting, but productivity analysis in governments has yet to advance beyond an embryonic stage.

Financing Difficulties

As unions contribute to the stress of the budgeting process they also add to that of the total fiscal situation. According to a variety of analyses, one-half to three-fourths of local government expenditures go to wages and benefits. "It is well to remember," says one analyst, "that more than 70 per cent of the operating budget of a typical local government is for personnel."[14] Another reminds us that personnel costs account for about three-fifths of New York's expense budget.[15] The exact proportion in the budget varies according to how capital costs and operating expenses are categorized, but employees clearly receive a major share of the money spent by cities and counties. And, as spending goes up, unions are naturally blamed for the increases because of their visibly aggressive tactics, particularly in fiscally strained governments.

Suppose a city has no surplus, is near the limit of its ability to tax property, and has a $100 million budget, of which $60 million is for personnel costs. Assume further that unions bargain (or lobby) successfully for a 6 percent increase in regular pay plus 2 percent of payroll in premium pay and fringe benefits. The result is a $4.8 million increase (plus other higher expenditures) that must be financed from higher yields, new taxes, or state aid. A large part of such an increase in personnel costs could occur even with-

14. James Marshall, "Management's Response to Public Employee Organizations," *California Public Employee Relations*, CPER Series No. 4 (January 1970), p. 3.
15. Netzer, "The Budget: Trends and Prospects," p. 660.

out unions, as was pointed out in Chapter 4, and still further increases would result from inflation and from greater workloads in city departments. But because unions are in the public spotlight, because they may strike or threaten to strike, city officials and the news media can point to union settlements as one cause of the increases.

UNION ATTITUDES

In bargaining sessions one of the important subjects discussed by management is the government's financial capacity or lack of it. Management bargainers may tell the unions, "We sympathize with your needs, but the city simply cannot afford the cost." This was the management position in Detroit in 1967 (drastically reversed the following year) and in Buffalo in 1968. Other managements play variations on this theme.

Depending on the locality and the sophistication of the group, unions respond differently, with reactions ranging anywhere from acceptance to defiance. In general they are losing whatever sympathy they may have had for management in its plight. Although editorial writers and politicians opposed to unions' demands may accuse them of driving the city or the county toward bankruptcy, unions know very well that the local government is not going to go out of business.[16] About the worst they can expect is a temporary taxpayers' revolt or the defeat of elected officials. They believe that the money they want is in the community somewhere. So more and more they are answering, "Finances are your problem. We expect fair pay and benefits and refuse to subsidize the government by accepting anything less."

While this is their general attitude, unions may listen to management's problems and help reduce the government's financial difficulties. The unions in Buffalo, for example, joined the city

16. Technically, cities *can* go bankrupt. Cities, counties, and other local taxing agencies can file petitions in federal bankruptcy courts under Chapter IX of the Bankruptcy Act to work out arrangements whereby they will pay their creditors less than 100 cents on the dollar. For obvious economic, public relations, and political reasons, such filings are rare. There were three in fiscal year 1968, none in 1969. (Administrative Office of the United States Courts, *Tables of Bankruptcy Statistics*, various years.)

government in requesting state aid and endorsed increased water rates and taxes; and employee organizations in Cincinnati campaigned for a proposed 1 percent payroll tax. St. Louis unions in 1969 consulted with civic groups on how city revenues could be raised. Employee groups in Detroit studied the city's books and lobbied for aid from the state. The American Federation of State, County, and Municipal Employees' (AFSCME) District Council 37 in New York agreed to help the mayors of the "big six" New York cities (New York City, Yonkers, Albany, Buffalo, Syracuse, and Rochester) lobby for more state support in 1970.[17] In other localities interviewees reported that unions tempered their demands according to the local fiscal situation. More recently the president of AFSCME addressed himself to the fiscal crisis of urban governments in a speech delivered at the annual meeting of the National League of Cities. Proposing assistance in developing educational programs on fiscal policy and tax reform, he also called for revenue sharing, full funding of existing programs, 100 percent federal financing of welfare and of categorical grants, increased federal grants for services (as opposed to capital items), and a special "emergency survival fund" for cities from which they can obtain more money to pay employees.[18] Thus, the political strength of this large union is being added to that of local government officials in urging remedial action by the federal government.

THE SITUATION IN VARIOUS GOVERNMENTS

The relationship of union pressures to urban finances can best be understood by examining a few key facts in several governments where the strain was evident. But while all serve to illustrate the problems, each case is unique, and only the most generalized conclusions can be drawn from intercity comparisons. The data from the several cities are not strictly comparable because of differences in the financial structures and in the methods of presenting figures in the budgets of the various governments.

17. Richard Phalon, " 'Big 6' Cities' Plea Gets Unions' Help but Governor's Opposition," *New York Times*, March 25, 1970.
18. Bureau of National Affairs, *Government Employee Relations Report*, No. 382 (Jan. 4, 1971), pp. B-1 to B-4.

Cincinnati. The city's expenditures rose by these amounts (in millions of dollars for fiscal years):[19]

	1968	*1969*	*Increase 1968–69*	*1970*	*Increase 1969–70*
Total budget	61.9	68.2	6.3 *(10.2%)*	74.5	6.3 *(9.2%)*
Personal services	39.0	41.6	2.6 *(6.7%)*	45.0	3.4 *(8.2%)*

Early in 1969, employees received a pay increase of 6 percent (the city had first offered 5 percent); but policemen and firemen got between 7 and 9 percent. A three-day strike of AFSCME members followed, as a result of misunderstandings and racial issues as well as pay, and was settled when the city increased its offer by 2 cents an hour for employees making up to $157.26 a week.[20] The increased costs were financed by increased yields from taxes, fines, fees, and other sources and by economies in services.

A more serious impasse in 1970 ended in a 34-day strike, also by AFSCME. (Policemen and firemen had already settled for a 10.7 percent increase in maximum annual pay from $8,807 to $9,752.) The city offered the AFSCME members 18 cents an hour or 5 percent, whichever was greater; they settled for a minimum raise of 22 cents, but 30 cents an hour for most of the categories of employees that had been on strike. The total cost of the wage adjustments plus related fringe benefits was estimated by the city finance director at $5.9 million on an annual basis, an increase of 14.2 percent in the personal services budget over 1969. This $5.9 million was $0.8 million more than the city council had provided on the basis of the city's offer; thus much of the increase was a direct result of the pressure of the strike.

This and other increases in the budget were paid for by a voter-approved increase in the city earnings tax from 1 percent to 1.7 percent, effective in June 1970. (Of this 0.7 percent increase, 0.15 percent must be used for capital improvements, and no more than 0.55 percent may be used for operating expenses.) It should be emphasized that the city budget was out of balance at the start of the fiscal year and that additional revenue was needed. The council had foreseen this need in 1968 and asked the voters for an in-

19. The source of this information is the "Tentative Annual Operating Budget of the City of Cincinnati, Ohio, for Fiscal Year 1971." Verified and corrected figures supplied by W. Donald Heisel by telephone Nov. 3, 1971. (This is the "All Funds" budget, less capital costs and debt service costs.)

20. For a full account see W. Donald Heisel, "Anatomy of a Strike," *Public Personnel Review*, Vol. 30 (October 1969), pp. 226–32.

crease in the city earnings tax to 2 percent, but the proposal had been defeated.[21]

Added pay and fringe benefits were a contributing cause of the budget increase in 1969 and a major cause in 1970. Only a small part of the increase was attributable directly to strike pressure. Most of it resulted from the city's policy of paying prevailing rates, regardless of its ability to find the funds. (If necessary, jobs are abolished to help finance the proper wage levels.) The presence of the unions obviously encourages such a policy.

San Francisco. The budget increases in San Francisco were as follows (in millions of dollars for fiscal years):[22]

	1968	*1969*	*Increase 1968–69*	*1970*	*Increase 1969–70*
Total budget	445.9	503.7	57.8 (*13.0%*)	598.6	94.9 (*18.8%*)
Personal services	232.8	265.1	32.3 (*13.9%*)	299.8	34.7 (*13.1%*)
Property tax rate	8.45%	9.73%	*15.20%*	*11.68%*	*20.00%*

Pay rates in San Francisco have been rising more slowly than the budget—5 percent for policemen and firemen, 7.9 percent for other employees in 1968; 12 percent for the former and 5 percent for the latter in 1969. Early in 1970, some 6,500 employees went on strike, and were supported by 7,000 others who honored picket lines and curtailed services. (There were about 22,000 employees in all.) The strikers were protesting a pay package recommended by the board of supervisors, which would have cost $3.8 million and provided raises of 2.5 to 5 percent. However, it would have eliminated a system under which new employees received automatic 5 percent annual pay raises during their first four years of employment. The nurses' association was also protesting the proposed elimination of pay differentials for city nurses over private employment rates. The board's proposal was well below the recommendation of the civil service commission, which would have given pay increases of 7.5 percent and cost some $9.5 million.

21. Letter from W. Donald Heisel, Institute of Governmental Research, University of Cincinnati, July 30, 1970.

22. These data were supplied by the Office of the Controller, City and County of San Francisco. Total budget figures exclude bonds funds. The tax rate includes that of the Unified School District tax, but excludes the San Francisco Bay Area Rapid Transit District tax.

The strike lasted four days, closing down public transportation and schools and disrupting other services. It was settled when the board of supervisors adopted a new pay package containing increases averaging 6 percent, restoring the automatic salary increments, and keeping the nurses' differentials. The cost was about $6.2 million instead of the $3.8 million originally contemplated.[23]

The difference between the offer and the settlement obviously represented an extremely small percentage of the budget. The impasse had resulted from the board of supervisors' reluctance to increase taxes enough to pay for the raise recommended by the civil service commission and from the unions' refusal to accept this judgment. The whole "crunch" took place without formalized, legally sanctioned collective bargaining.

Detroit. Increases in Detroit were of this magnitude (in millions of dollars for fiscal years):[24]

	1968	*1969*	*Increase 1968–69*	*1970*	*Increase 1969–70*
Total appropriations	322.4	354.3	31.9 (*9.9%*)	404.9	50.6 (*14.3%*)
Personal services	152.6	177.7	25.1 (*16.4%*)	195.7	18.0 (*10.1%*)
Property tax rate	*23.97%*	*24.07%*		*24.15%*	

In submitting the fiscal year 1969 budget to the common council, the mayor emphasized that employees had not been given a pay raise in two years and proposed a package of increases that would cost over $22 million, and would cover all employees paid from tax funds. This clearly made up the greater part of the increase shown in the first line of the table above. The pay raises, which amounted to about 14 percent for employees other than police and firemen and 19 percent for the latter, were in effect paid for by an increase of from 1 to 2 percent in the income tax on city residents, which yielded some $29 million.

An important factor was the impasse over police salaries, dis-

23. Data are from Bureau of National Affairs, *Government Employee Relations Report*, No. 340 (March 16, 1970), p. B-10, No. 341 (March 23, 1970), p. B-7, and *New York Times*, March 17, 1970.

24. Data are from *City of Detroit, Budget for Maintenance and Improvement Purposes, Fiscal Year Ending June 30, 1970*, and preceding issues. They cover tax-supported activities and do *not* include appropriations for aviation, housing, parking, transit, water, and sewage disposal.

cussed in Chapter 4. The fact-finding panel, invited by both parties to suggest sources of funds for any increase they might recommend, reported

that the City had the legal authority to raise substantially more money from property taxes than it elected to raise, and that this added revenue would have been adequate to finance a significant salary increase at least for police officers. In other words, the City's alleged inability to pay increased police salaries is in some measure a self-imposed inability.[25]

The panel then suggested some sources of funds for police salaries: otherwise unused salary funds, increased fines for traffic violations, a 5 percent "savings" or accrual program, use of the city's share of state income tax revenues, and, finally, deficit financing.[26] The actual content of these suggestions is less significant than the fact that they represented incursion by a labor relations panel into difficult problems of public finance.

The following year, when pay raises were 4 percent for policemen and firemen and 9 percent for others, there were no new revenue sources to finance the higher expenditures. The mayor recommended an increase in the property tax, but this was rejected by the common council, resulting in a reduction of estimated revenue of approximately $15.4 million. This sum was replaced by other budgeted revenues, including a repayment by the water board to the general fund for debt service for sewer construction amounting to $10 million, $3 million from the sale of city-owned acreage, and an anticipated recovery of $1 million in a drug antitrust suit. Nevertheless, these moneys did not materialize by the end of the fiscal year, and there was an operating deficit of $20 million, which was met by issuing tax anticipation notes.

Financial troubles continued into fiscal 1971. Remedial measures included increased state aid, an increase in the property tax to the statutory limit, an excise tax on utility bills, and a temporary layoff of more than five hundred employees. The mayor asked employees to work forty hours a week instead of the official thirty-five, but unions waged a successful court battle to prevent this.

In short, increased personnel costs resulting from bargaining

25. Ronald W. Haughton, Charles C. Killingsworth, and Russell A. Smith, "Findings and Recommendations on Unresolved Economic and Other Issues" (Detroit Police Dispute Panel, Feb. 27, 1968; processed), p. 17.

26. *Ibid.*, pp. 19–20.

have been responsible in large measure for expenditure increases, and there has been continuing difficulty in finding the money to pay for them.

New York. The largest budget of all showed trends like the others (in millions of dollars for fiscal years):[27]

	1968	*1969*	*Increase 1968–69*	*1970*	*Increase 1969–70*
Expense budget	5,242.3	6,006.6	764.3 (*14.6%*)	6,604.0	597.4 (*9.9%*)
Personal services		(Generally estimated at *60%* of the budget expense.)			

The mayor's budget messages indicate that personnel costs were a larger part of the second increase than of the first—$400 million in fiscal 1970 and $230 million in fiscal 1969. As in most of the cities studied, it is impossible to relate these increases directly to union pressures. Still, the multiplicity of bargaining units, their aggressiveness, and the differences in bargaining periods strongly suggest that the unions obtained more than unorganized employees could have, particularly in a period of fiscal strain.

The budget was balanced with great difficulty in both years through operating economies; increased property tax yields, aided by the revised computation of equalization rates authorized by the state legislature; increased revenue from local income and other special city taxes; and rising aid from the federal and state governments. The mayor exerted particular pressure to have state aid increased. This was successful in fiscal 1969, when state aid totaled $1,611 million, due in part to a new Emergency Aid for Cities program,[28] but the state budget for the following year provided an increase of only about 2 percent for New York City.

Facing another large deficit in fiscal 1971, the city had to delay submitting its budget to the legislature by a month beyond the statutory date. After considering a wide variety of revenue ideas from the city, the legislature approved a package that included

27. The data were obtained from *The City of New York, Message of the Mayor, Accompanying the Submission of the Executive Budget for the Fiscal Year 1969–1970 to the Board of Estimate and the City Council,* and *Message . . . for 1968–1969.* The Estimate for Personal Services was supplied by the Director of Personnel for New York City, June 18, 1970. For a clear and comprehensive analysis of New York City's financial problem, see Netzer, "The Budget: Trends and Prospects," pp. 651–714.

28. David Bernstein, "Financing the City Government," in *Governing the City: Challenges and Options for New York* (Academy of Political Science, 1969), p. 84.

taxes on commercial rents, hotel charges, and automobile use; extension of the city sales tax to include parking fees; and an authorization for the city to establish off-track horse race betting facilities. Most significantly, revenue sharing by the state was clarified and increased. Cities and counties in New York State are to receive 21 percent of the state income taxes collected in their areas—which will mean a $158 million increase in state aid to New York City—and one-third of the state lottery proceeds over $26 million.[29]

Dayton. The general fund budget in Dayton has risen at a declining rate. The amounts (in millions of dollars for calendar years) are:[30]

	1968	*1969*	*Increase 1968–69*	*1970*	*Increase 1969–70*
General fund	26.3	29.6	3.3 (*12.5%*)	31.4	1.8 (*6.1%*)
Personal services	*77.4%* of general fund			*80%* of general fund (est.)	

In 1968 the unions in Dayton bargained for and received moderate pay increases of 5 to about 7 percent (see Table 5 in Chapter 4). These raises added about $1 million to the 1969 budget according to the estimate of one official interviewed. The total increased cost of personal services that year (including nonbargained pay increases and fringe benefit escalations tied to all the pay raises) was $2.3 million[31]—obviously a large part of the total increase in the general fund. This occurred at a time when the budget was balanced only by cutting budget requests (no new programs and no substantial increases in old ones) and by drawing on trust funds.[32]

The city management proposed to relieve the strain by increasing the local income tax rate from 1.0 to 1.5 percent. One top offi-

29. Richard Phalon, "$400-Million Albany Tax Plan Expected to Ease City's Plight," *New York Times,* April 21, 1970.

30. Data are from *Financial Report, 1968: Dayton, Action City* (City of Dayton, Division of Accounting, Department of Finance, 1969), p. 20; "1970–74 Financial Plan, City of Dayton" (processed), supplemented by telephone inquiry. The figure for 1968 is the audited total. The 1969 figure is estimated. The figure for 1970 is the amount that was budgeted for that year.

31. "Tax Budget, Dayton, Ohio, 1969" (Office of the City Manager, July 10, 1968; processed), p. 5.

32. City manager's budget message, "Recommended Operating Budget for 1969," Dec. 18, 1968, in *1969 Budget and Programs, Dayton, Ohio* (City of Dayton, Office of the City Manager, 1968), p. ii.

cial said that the bargained pay raises were contingent on approval by voters of this tax increase and that the city could reopen the agreement. The referendum failed in May 1969, but the agreement was not disturbed. The city "got by" through economies—refraining from purchasing needed equipment and from filling vacant jobs. Some revenues were also diverted from capital to operating purposes because a later referendum in the same year reauthorized the 1 percent tax but removed a requirement that 15 percent of the proceeds be used for capital purposes. The latter change released some $2 million for the operating budget.

Policemen and firemen (the former after prolonged negotiation and the participation of a federal mediator) agreed to a two-year contract in 1970, which provided a 6.2 percent pay increase retroactive to the end of 1969, 4.8 percent in June 1970, and 4.6 percent in December 1970.[33] Higher union demands and a renewed effort to raise the income tax are expected in the future.

Here again city officials who believe in collective bargaining and in paying fair prevailing rates are having trouble getting enough funds from taxpayers to pay the agreed-upon wages and fringe benefits.

St. Louis. The budget increases in St. Louis (shown below in millions of dollars for fiscal years) reflected principally increased salary levels:[34]

	1968	*1969*	*Increase 1968–69*	*1970*	*Increase 1969–70*
Expenditures	95.3	100.4	5.1 (*5.4%*)	109.6	9.2 (*9.2%*)
Personal services	71.1	75.5	4.4 (*6.2%*)	81.0	5.5 (*7.3%*)

33. Bureau of National Affairs, *Government Employee Relations Report*, No. 350 (May 25, 1970).

34. Data are from "Proposed Appropriations Recommended by Board of Estimate and Apportionment for Fiscal Year 1970–71, together with Comparative Expenditures for the Two Years Next Preceding (1969–70 and 1968–69)," tabulation from Division of the Budget, City of St. Louis (July 30, 1970); "City of St. Louis, Budget Recommendations for the Fiscal Year 1969–70 as Submitted to the Board of Aldermen by the Board of Estimate and Apportionment, June 6, 1969" (processed). Figures are for total municipal revenue budget, comprising both city-controlled and state-controlled departments.

In order to obtain additional tax collections, the end of the fiscal year 1969 was moved from March 31 to April 30. For comparability, the figures shown for total expenditures and for personal services, which for the thirteen-month period were $109.1 million for total expenditures and $81.5 million for personal services, were adjusted to a twelve-month basis, as shown for that year.

The 1969 pay increase in St. Louis, which amounted to 5 to 10 percent, did not take effect until August 17, 1969, because of financing difficulties. Impatient over the delay, refuse division workers struck for thirteen days. The increase would have cost $5.1 million on an annual basis but cost less than this for fiscal 1970 because it went into effect three and a half months after the fiscal year began. Even so, it was hard to finance. Efforts to obtain state aid were in vain, but the legislature did pass a law permitting cities to levy a 1 percent sales tax. This levy then had to be approved by St. Louis voters. It was made part of an "anti-crime" referendum package, which also included proposed bond issues for improved street lighting and for a facility for juvenile delinquents. The voters approved the tax in March 1970, with collections beginning July 1, 1970. This sales tax is expected to yield about $20 million a year.

Increased costs between the effective dates of the pay raise and of the new tax were met in several ways: by economies (cutting the work force by approximately 500 jobs through attrition), by an occupational tax on various types of businesses, and by the accelerated collection of taxes on utility bills.

Unions were consulted on these fiscal problems and showed understanding, but their pressure for increases, based on continuing inflation and on real needs of their members, was unrelenting.

Other Indicators. These six cases illustrate the strains that have appeared and the remedies that have been adopted. More can be found in other cities and counties. For example,

BUFFALO. Most of an $8 million budget increase in one fiscal year (1969) and half of a $4.5 increase in the next resulted from bargaining. Property taxes went up, and state aid became more generous.

LOS ANGELES COUNTY. "Wages in the community have risen 5.9% over the past year, and this requires $24.7 million additional in property tax levy to cover salary increases for County employees."[35]

PHILADELPHIA. The city wage tax was raised from 2 to 3 percent after substantial wage increases were granted to city employees.

NEW ORLEANS. A new charge for sanitation service had to be imposed to pay for wage increases.

35. *Recommendations for the Proposed 1969–70 Budget*, Presented to the Board of Supervisors by the Chief Administrative Officer (County of Los Angeles, California, 1969), p. iv.

MILWAUKEE. Some $6 million of a $13 million budget increase (1967–68) can be attributed to negotiated pay increases. The tax rate and various fees for services were raised.

Revenues for Raises. Negotiated (or otherwise pressured) increases in pay and benefits are major factors in pushing up local government budgets. There is as yet no proof that budgets are raised more by unions than they would be otherwise, but this is probable. Without union pressures, city and county officials would be more successful in holding down the costs that have become so difficult to finance. Yet more and more officials find themselves looking for money in order to raise employees' pay and benefits. Both unions and labor experts are having an increasingly important effect on public finance decisions. Unions, like revenue specialists, know that the money is "there" somewhere in the community or the state. The problem is how much can be raised and by what means. Management contentions that the city or county "can't afford it" are becoming less and less acceptable. The Detroit police fact finders disagreed with the city's claim that there was no money for police salary increases. The Buffalo policemen's union also went to fact-finding in 1968 and won 5 percent more in pay than the city had been willing to give them.

Similar events were occurring in cities not included in this study. Arbitration panels in Pittsburgh decided on pay hikes for policemen and firemen that city officials said might make it necessary to raise real estate taxes from 46 to 60 mills on land and from 23 to 30 mills on buildings.[36] They actually did increase the millage by 9 on land and 4.5 on buildings, effective January 1, 1970, as well as increasing a tax on parking.[37]

As another example, a fact-finding panel studying police pay raises in Portland, Oregon, considered the city's shaky fiscal situation at length and suggested

amending the City Charter to raise the 6 percent limitation on property tax, adoption of a City income tax, a payroll tax, or a sales tax. The panel reminded the city that it could impose a hotel-motel occupancy tax which would not demand voter approval.[38]

36. *New York Times,* Nov. 17, 1968.
37. Information by telephone from City of Pittsburgh budget staff, Aug. 14, 1970.
38. Bureau of National Affairs, *Government Employee Relations Report,* No. 337 (Feb. 23, 1970), p. B-12.

These are extraordinary events in public finance and political science. Labor fact finders in the public sector are substituting their judgment for that of elected legislators and executives concerning the nature and productivity of local government revenue sources. This means that they will devise and try to implement standards of acceptable revenue effort. One practitioner, in a trailblazing article, suggests a method of reaching decisions by "comparing its [the community's] ability to pay, measured by its taxable resources, and the amount of tax revenues which actually have been collected and spent on services" (for example, the particular services under scrutiny).[39] He proposes analyses of measures of wealth and the tax structure of the community concerned.

Fact finders are now being joined by arbitrators. The Michigan and Pennsylvania statutes already provide for compulsory arbitration for policemen and firemen. Fact finders, mediators, and arbitrators are likely to be advancing more and more into areas formerly occupied only by economists. The latter can be of great assistance to the labor experts by continuing to refine measures of relative tax effort and by further developing program budgeting techniques.

Whether or not local governments are involved in impasse procedures, their finances will be in critical condition. They will surely be forced to seek additional revenue hurriedly and under strong pressure from unions, as well as from other claimants. But the supplementary revenue sources they find may be inadequate expedients, and the pressures are not going to lessen. There is no satisfactory solution short of heroic local tax reform plus effective plans to share more state revenue and particularly more federal revenue with the cities and counties. Both steps face formidable political and technical obstacles.

Handing the Money to Departments

Unionism has had little effect on budget execution, except to put more emphasis on its restrictive aspects. The typical department head in a local government is not always free to spend his

39. David B. Ross, "The Arbitration of Public Employee Wage Disputes," *Industrial and Labor Relations Review,* Vol. 23 (October 1969), p. 6.

budgeted funds as he wishes. His spending may be controlled by the chief executive (or really by the budget staff) to be sure that money (1) is spent for the purposes for which the legislative body intended it, (2) is not spent in excess of the amounts designated for each purpose, (3) is not invested in "foolish" or "unnecessary" projects, and (4) is so managed that the executive has some flexibility in meeting emergencies.[40]

As the urban fiscal crisis deepens, it is increasingly important to a chief executive that money be saved out of the expense budget to meet unexpected or hard-to-plan-for problems: floods, riots, blizzards, sudden influxes of poor people. Now union settlements must be added to the list—settlements after the budget is submitted, settlements costing more than the budget provides, settlements after strikes.

Yet stringent controls are not yet universal. In nearly half of the governments studied, a department head is usually free to spend his budgeted funds as passed by the legislative body.

Among the cities and counties that reported having taken belt-tightening measures, Detroit, Multnomah County, and Tacoma reported instances of cuts in services or delays in filling jobs or in purchasing equipment. "But it's a losing fight," said one Detroit official. "How can you sit on some requisition for personnel or equipment for the police department or a city hospital?"

Other cities imposed more general "freezes" on appointments, purchases, use of overtime, or travel expenses in order to be sure that they could meet their budgets. Buffalo, for example, delayed planned expansions in several departments; Hartford postponed street repairs, as well as many other types of expense; and Philadelphia cut library and trash collection service without causing strong public reactions. Philadelphia also set up a "freeze board," whose members—the finance director, the managing director, and the mayor himself—must approve the filling of any job vacancies. The St. Louis government cut its purchases substantially, and New Orleans officials curtailed library hours and street repair work.

---

40. See Jesse Burkhead, *Government Budgeting* (Wiley, 1956), Chap. 13, "Budget Execution," pp. 340–56. Also, for a discussion of restrictive budget administration in state governments (which differ little in these respects from large city governments), see Allen Schick, "Control Patterns in State Budget Execution," *Public Administration Review*, Vol. 24 (June 1968), pp. 97–106.

In budget execution, as in other functions, New York is a special case. That city's extreme difficulty in budgeting for personnel costs in times of fiscal despair has been noted above. Its finance officials contend that these circumstances emphasize the necessity of the city's longstanding practice of "forced accruals." These

were adopted as a conscious economy procedure during the Great Depression. This system of personnel savings by not filling vacancies in authorized positions, first used as an emergency measure, has since become an established part of City budget and personnel administration. Under this system each department and agency is forced to realize predetermined personnel savings below annual budgeted amounts. Normally, a department achieves some of this through resignations, retirements, or death of employees. But additional accruals are imposed on top of these "normal savings" as a budget-balancing device.[41]

Such a device is viewed with dismay by advocates of more decentralized administration, who contend that city departments *can* operate more speedily and effectively, and no more expensively, without such centralized monitoring.[42]

Forced economies in New York and in the other governments mentioned above are not evenly applied because the functions of some departments are more critical than those of others. Police departments are exempted or are affected only lightly, as are hospitals. And in Hartford, where in 1968 the city government ordered a freeze on filling jobs, the social services department, which was struggling under a wave of Puerto Rican immigrants, received favored treatment.

Unions can generally be expected to resist economy measures. As was pointed out in Chapter 5, they exert strong pressure against both staff cutting and keeping staff below the strength authorized by law. Often this pressure is well rationalized: city hospital patients must have better care; streets must be safer; welfare recipients must live with dignity. In two cities the rationalization sought to put human above bird or animal values. Why spend public

---

41. Temporary Commission on City Finances, *Better Financing for New York City,* Final Report of the Temporary Commission on City Finances Including the First, Second, and Third Reports and Additional Materials (City of New York, 1966), pp. 72–73.

42. *Ibid.,* p. 73. See also Joseph Pois, "Personnel Implications of New York City's Budget Process," in David T. Stanley, *Professional Personnel for the City of New York* (Brookings Institution, 1963), pp. 357–71.

money for a penguin house (Detroit) or an incubator for a baby gorilla (Cincinnati) when services to citizens and pay for employees are inadequately financed?

Conclusion

Unions affect both the process and the content of local government budgets. As unions gain strength and as bargaining units burgeon, the negotiating process (whether it is formalized collective bargaining or not) becomes more complex, more time-consuming, and more likely to drag beyond budget deadlines. Realistic budgeting is also handicapped by retroactive pay provisions in union agreements. All this means uncertainty about how much of the available resources will be spent for (or absorbed by) inadequately foreseen personnel costs, or how much new resources will be needed. If there is delay in finding resources, as there was in New York and St. Louis, the process is lengthened further. The total effect is obviously damaging to efficient use of the budget as an instrument of rational choice among program priorities. And, as was noted above, unions contribute to the pressure on local governments to find new and expanded revenue sources.

Despite these effects both union and government officials regard budget and finance as management functions. There is only scattered evidence that unions are helping local officials to obtain aid from higher levels of government or to make their own revenue systems more productive. In only a few instances have the impressive political power and tactical position of the unions been used in efforts to achieve more effective local tax measures and more satisfactory systems of intergovernmental fiscal relations.

CHAPTER SEVEN

The Impact in General: Present and Prospective

Urban public administration is undergoing major changes as a result of union pressures. A "whole new ball game" has started since unions in the public sector have begun to operate in areas traditionally reserved to management. While the force of the union impact varies by locality (it is greater in New York than in New Orleans) and by function (it has more influence in grievance procedures than in civil service testing methods), the central fact is change, and the rate of change is increasing. Pay, benefits, and working conditions are more and more being determined bilaterally, and the scope of union agreements is expanding significantly. Already, painful public finance problems are being complicated and aggravated by union pressures.

Behind the changes is growing power based on the sheer size and aggressiveness of the unions. More than a million local government employees are union members, and for the most part they are led by experienced (though thinly spread) full-time labor professionals. Their power takes several forms. First, unions are large political blocs, representing or influencing enough votes to decide a reasonably close municipal election. Their influence is greater if they ally themselves with other interest groups for various purposes. It is greater yet when union members are personally acquainted with political leaders.

Second, and even more important, unions can close down a city, or at least some of its services. In the mind of many a union leader and city official, the possibility of a strike or slowdown is at the heart of the union–management relationship. Although antistrike laws are nearly universal, unions in local governments *do* strike, and frequently they do so with the advantage on their side and with impunity. The presence of employees on the job is the main bargaining weapon of the unions.

Two other aspects of union power are less important nationwide but may be of crucial importance in some localities. One is the time-honored strength of labor solidarity. Unions in the private sector can—and do—join with those in local governments for political action, and they can—and do—balk at crossing picket lines around city hospitals and dumps. Finally, some unions, notably the Service Employees International Union (SEIU) and the American Federation of State, County, and Municipal Employees (AFSCME), are a means of gaining better economic conditions for black, Spanish-speaking, or other disadvantaged citizens, and their power in turn reflects the support of those elements of the community.[1]

Thus unions are in a position of strength, with no weakening in sight. Persons opposed to this development regard it as a threat to the traditional governmental system—a reduction in the power of elected representatives. Yet the unions' power can also be looked upon as a correction of the previously weak status of employees. Their gains can also be thought of as adding strength to one form of citizen influence on government. For decades mayors and city councils have been blocked or stimulated by chambers of commerce, bar associations, sewer contractors, taxpayers' leagues, and even gambling syndicates. The city bureaucracies, at first poorly organized, have been a growing force in the contest for power and resources, as Sayre and Kaufman, and Banfield and Wilson,[2] and others have pointed out. Now their strength is more effectively institutionalized and exerted at almost every level of management.

1. This can also be a weakening factor because many union members may actually oppose such efforts, as was noted in Chap. 3.

2. Wallace S. Sayre and Herbert Kaufman, *Governing New York City* (Russell Sage Foundation, 1960), especially Chaps. 7–11; and Edward C. Banfield and James Q. Wilson, *City Politics* (Harvard University Press, 1963), Chap. 15.

In short, democratic governments respond to interest groups, and employee unions are interest groups that are strong because of their internal position as well as their external political power and alliances.

Even though the nineteen governments in this study were chosen for variety in their location, size, form of government, and civil service traditions, these factors proved to have little effect on the ways in which unions relate to public administration. Differences among the localities were due primarily to labor relations history—the size and numbers of unions, and the way they were dealt with by successive councils, chief executives, budget officers, and personnel officers. Essentially, the operating styles and personalities of union and management spokesmen were the major variables. Another intercity difference is equally obvious: administrative difficulties increase at least in proportion to the number of bargaining units and are kept in check only by strong determination on the part of management to keep personnel policies and benefits consistent.

Chapters 2 through 6 reviewed the impact of the unions' strength on personnel administration, on work supervision, and on financial management. In this chapter the impact on various levels of government is summarized, possible limits on the use of union power to influence city management are discussed, and some guidelines are offered for administration in the future.

Effect on Administration of Local Governments

It was not unusual for government officials and civic observers who were interviewed for this study to raise such questions as "What is happening to government achievements under union pressures? Do unions impair government's ability to translate the will of the people into effective action?" This study was not designed to provide answers in terms of the quality and quantity of government services—such as cubic yards of trash removed, thoroughness of prenatal health examinations, or rigor and frequency of building inspections. But judging by specific bargaining outcomes, by interviews, by government reports, and by press reactions, the answer to such questions is "not much." Some forces tend to offset each other. For example, unions can impair efficiency in a strongly organized department if they accelerate cost increases and if they insist on work rules and conditions that hinder the flexible use of managerial techniques. On the other hand, unions may improve program effectiveness by demanding that the organization be adequately staffed, by pressing for equal levels of service throughout the city, or by insisting on a sound safety program. The work performance of employees may also be aided by the psychological security resulting from an effective grievance procedure and good fringe benefits, or it may be hindered by knowledge that desirable assignments are based on seniority rather than performance.

In general, according to testimony by department heads and other executives, major policy choices about what programs shall be carried on are not affected by union pressures. However, decisions on levels of program effort are beginning to be affected as a result of the financial strains that have been discussed above.

LEGISLATIVE BODIES AND CHIEF EXECUTIVES

Mainly "what is happening" to local government is that both legislative bodies and chief executives are *more preoccupied with union matters* and are *more limited in their discretion to manage.* As for preoccupation, if a strike occurs or seems imminent, the mayor or manager and the city council pay little attention to anything else. With an eye on finances, public relations, political support, and the state capital, they are involved in day and night maneuvers. Furthermore, they must make detailed plans to administer the government under strike conditions.

Councils and mayors or managers are also equally concerned when collective bargaining (or "meet and confer") reaches a climax without a strike threat because they still may be confronted by a crisis of finance, or public relations, or interunion rivalry.

Even in noncrisis situations involving unions, more time, manpower, and overhead expense must be devoted to personnel problems than would otherwise be necessary. Union delegations visit councilmen and the chief executive; the latter finds his relationships with the council more complex; and both the legislators and the executive must delve into labor relations problems with the personnel staff and with department heads. Furthermore, management's preoccupations are multiplied when it must deal with dozens of unions, as in Boston and Milwaukee, or with hundreds, as in New York. In summary, the management effort is invariably more tense, more time-consuming, more public than that applied to nonunion personnel problems, because of the adversary posture of the unions and their generally aggressive attitudes.

Many ways in which the unions limit management's discretion have been brought out in earlier chapters. Probably most important to councils, mayors, and managers is the fact that their operating budgets are less controllable than they formerly were. Decisions on personnel costs—which are more than half the budgeted expenses—are made bilaterally rather than by management alone. Moreover the process takes so long, especially if there is an impasse, that the budget becomes open-ended. This aggravates the already critical problem of raising revenues.

Another significant limitation involves management's surrender of part of its discretion in settling grievances and administering discipline. The growing, but still minor, influence of unions in classifying jobs and assigning work has also been noted. Less frequent but still significant is union participation in determining program policies,[3] as in the New York City social services situation. Rare but full of implications for the future is the use of union power to force a public official out of office. This was demonstrated in February 1970, when Philadelphia trashmen conducted a slowdown that ended in the resignation of a newly appointed streets department commissioner. (The appointee had been a police officer, and the employees preferred a professional engineer or someone from their own department.)

CENTRAL MANAGEMENT AGENCIES

The impact of unions on central management agencies (personnel and budget staffs in particular) is complex. In cities where a labor relations office has been set up, the personnel and budget

3. See discussion below of the scope of bargaining, pp. 145–48.

staffs may lose authority and functions. Clearly this has happened in Detroit and New York. Whether or not such an office has been established, the personnel and budget staffs, like the legislative bodies and chief executives, are busier than ever, and their policy choices are substantially reduced. If the personnel or civil service director still has responsibility for union relations, he generally spends at least half of his time on it. If there is a separate labor relations specialist, the personnel director has to consult with him on classification, pay, and grievances—many of the matters that the unions bring to either one of them. Discretion is reduced, as has been pointed out above repeatedly, because so many of the terms of employment are bargained and decided jointly, instead of being determined by management. Those decisions that management makes unilaterally (such as job classification or eligibility for premium pay) are considered under the eye of a critical union representative.

Budget staffs that may have worked in the pattern of traditional public administration can look back with nostalgic incredulity. For now their game is more complex, more difficult, more public. Timetables are threatened, reserves disappear, and revenues become inadequate.

DEPARTMENT HEADS

Generally, department heads also must give more frequent and more intense attention to personnel matters because of the unions. To begin with, they must spend time on negotiations. In some places (as in Hartford) department heads may be formal members of the city's negotiating team; in others (Detroit and New York) they bargain supplemental agreements with the unions on matters relating to their own departments. But their most frequent role is to "back up" the management negotiators with information about the potential effect of changes in pay, fringes, and working conditions in their departments.

These executives—the sanitation director, the hospital administrator, the public works chief—spend even more time on such day-to-day matters as determining assignments, allocating the use of equipment, and adjusting minor grievances, all of which are decided under the provisions of agreements, under union scrutiny, and often with union consultation. But by and large, the department heads interviewed did not object to this state of affairs. They commended the unions both for their influence in keeping management alert and careful and for their ability to secure gains for employees. However, they repeatedly emphasized the need for supervisors to become more competent and mature in handling on-the-job relationships.

Another effect is that tight-fisted budget execution (a general necessity, as was noted in Chapter 6) may also curtail the department heads' flexibility in managing freely within their budgets.

In order to make the point, the contrast between management under union pressures and management without them has been overemphasized. Administrators have never had an entirely free rein. They are hemmed in by laws, rules, and financial restrictions. Elected or politically appointed officials always scrutinize, and sometimes interfere with, their work. They must share their authority with civil service commissions, fair employment committees, and various other boards and councils. Moreover, they are subject to employee pressures and objections even without unions. Now, in a highly unionized situation, their freedom to manage is also limited but more clearly, intensely, and systematically than before.

Effect on State Governments

The impact of local government unions is strongly felt by all three branches of state government as well. Legislatures, after long study and controversy, have enacted public employee relations statutes and have amended them later. Legislative consideration of local government revenue measures and state aid appropriations is treated with special urgency and sensitivity because of union pressures. In the state courts, new law is being made as judges decide suits on public labor issues and rule on requests for injunctions to halt strikes. Assuming a more active role, albeit reluctantly, they have issued contempt citations and have fined or imprisoned union leaders who refuse to comply with court orders.

The executive branches of state governments are involved at several levels. Governors, personally concerned with the wisdom and political adroitness of their labor policies, must make difficult choices, especially when disputes threaten health or safety. Should the governor of New York have the National Guard pick up garbage in New York City? How much protection should the governor of South Carolina give to hospital strikebreakers? State governments also maintain staffs to administer the employee relations laws. They issue regulations on representation, bargaining, and labor practices and may furnish fact finders, mediators, and arbitrators to local governments and unions locked in impasse situations. In all these areas of concern, state governments can expect increasing workloads and challenging policy problems.

Are There Limits to Unions' Power in Administration?

The power of government employee unions has been distressing to some commentators:

The most powerful communities in the nation now seem most powerless when confronted by the defiance of the minority and the helplessness of the law and the majority. And the defiance of the minority is now spreading to government employes.[4]

and:

The community cannot tolerate the notion that it is defenseless at the hands of organized workers to whom it has entrusted responsibility for essential services.[5]

Behind such consternation three kinds of concerns are evident: (1) realization that illegal strikes are growing in number; (2) fear that negotiated agreements (with or without strikes) will give utterly extravagant pay and benefits to employees; and (3) fear that unions will "take over" policy formulation and major administrative decision making.

On the first point, the legality, propriety, and/or necessity of strikes are beyond the scope of this study; other books in this Brookings series deal with the processes and the laws relevant to impasse

4. James Reston in *New York Times*, March 20, 1970.
5. A. H. Raskin, "The Revolt of the Civil Servants," *Saturday Review*, Vol. 51 (Dec. 7, 1968), p. 89.

resolution, strikes, and sanctions.[6] It is simply stated here that, on the one hand, strikes have inconvenienced the public and have probably increased government costs, but, on the other hand, they have also corrected injustices, secured gains for employees, and been a major cause of change in public administration.

LIMITS ON EXCESSIVE SETTLEMENTS

What will avert utter extravagance? What will prevent a salary of $30,000 for fire fighters, a twenty-four-hour week for audit clerks, a two-month paid vacation for hospital attendants? The answers lie in the realities of our political system and of the bargaining process. Unions in politics are strong but by no means invincible, especially in the largest cities, where they are only one of many factors in the decision process.[7] Unions that abandon all restraint know that they will seriously jeopardize friendships at city hall and in the wards; and their actions will very likely encourage the rise of political opposition. Moreover, other powerful blocs of the citizenry may not only make certain that the demands of the unions are denied but may curtail union power by legislation. Finally, the possibility of punitive or restrictive action by the state government is ever present. Union aggressiveness will therefore stop short of these points and has done so thus far. As was shown in Chapter 4, unions have achieved financial gains that are not excessive.

One caveat should be mentioned. Feelings of unreasoning helplessness, anger, and despair occur among all groups contesting for municipal power and resources. It is perfectly possible for union members—perhaps more so than for union leaders—to seek extravagant objectives for emotional rather than rational economic reasons.

In the bargaining process unions are necessarily restrained by prevailing practice in the private sector and in other governments, by fiscal realities, by the need to do business in the future with

6. Harry H. Wellington and Ralph K. Winter, Jr., *The Unions and the Cities* (Brookings Institution, 1971), especially Pt. 4. John F. Burton, Jr., and Arnold R. Weber are also studying this aspect of collective bargaining in the public sector.

7. Charles R. Adrian, "Governing Megacentropolis: The Politics," *Public Administration Review*, Vol. 30 (September/October 1970), p. 499.

management, by management's skill and resolution in bargaining, by impasse resolution procedures, and by management's ultimate willingness to "take a strike" and apply sanctions.

In summary, recent history suggests that the gains of the unions have not been excessive. There will be efforts in the future to get more, and both the political and procedural restraints will be burdened, but disastrous outcomes are hardly likely.

LIMITS ON SHARING POLICY AND MANAGERIAL AUTHORITY

What keeps unions from taking over management completely? Will they determine program policies, plan work methods, decide what equipment will be acquired, assume command of the entire personnel process? In general, the answers have to be negative because of the nature of the political process and the union-management relationship. Constitutions, charters, laws, and political traditions require that governments be run by officials chosen by citizens to be responsible for results. Unions recognize this. They do not want the responsibility of running a community, with its multiple pressures for setting priorities, innovation, compromise, and maximum utilization of inadequate resources. They need an adversary—someone to make demands of, to criticize, to push against. They need someone else to be "management," so that they can be "labor."

Yet management needs to show strength. If elected and appointed officials do not take a strong, positive view of their authority and responsibilities, they will find them significantly reduced by unions. On this point, some remarks before the United States Conference of Mayors by Arvid Anderson, Chairman of the New York City Office of Collective Bargaining, are pertinent:

> As one who has spent a considerable part of his professional life at the bargaining table, in both the private and public sectors, I have noticed a marked distinction in the attitudes of the public official toward what he believes he has the authority to do and what his counterpart in the private sector believes he can do.
>
> It has been my general experience that public administrators think they can do only what they are expressly authorized to do and in the absence of such authority they will not act.
>
> The private manager, the private lawyer does not think in these terms. He thinks in terms of whether the action proposed is wise or un-

wise. Whether he wants to take the action is another question. But he assumes that unless specifically prohibited he has the authority to act.

Attorneys for the unions and union representatives do not think in terms of inhibitions on their ability to act.

I recognize that there are real fiscal and legal restraints on the ability of some local governments to accommodate collective bargaining concepts and procedures to existing state and municipal laws. But lawyers and public officials can figure out how to get things done as well as how not to take action.[8]

Still, many a public official will not want to display this amount of strength. Even if he does, he may be inhibited by legal restrictions, by fear of legal reprisals, and by political constraints.

Program Policy. On the whole, unions have not tried thus far to determine basic program policy. There are some exceptions. Social service unions have advocated the liberalization of welfare policies and benefits. Police unions have supported strong crowd control policies and preventive detention of criminal suspects, while fire fighters' groups have quarreled over coverage of high-risk areas. And (as an illustration from outside this study) teachers' unions have become interested in class size, disciplinary standards, and decentralization of school administration. These examples can be related in varying degree to the material benefit and job satisfaction of the union members, and it is likely that most future incursions into broad policy areas will be similarly motivated.

Bargainable Work Management. Turning to the planning and management of work operations, the line between what is bargainable and what is subject to management decision is not easy to draw. Unions have bargained an end to split shifts in hospitals, but general scheduling is a management prerogative. Trashmen's unions have negotiated for gloves and raincoats, but management generally retains the right to decide whether a new compacting truck shall be bought. Yet such management prerogatives, even if they are grounded in laws and rights clauses, can be negotiated on the basis of their effect on employees and can be upset by strike threats or by political action by unions. Hence the line between the bargainable and the "decidable" varies according to the basic rules and politics of the situation. Unions do not assume complete

8. Arvid Anderson, "Statement," in Wilbur H. Baldinger (ed.), *City Problems of 1970, Proceedings, 1970 Annual Conference, United States Conference of Mayors* (Washington, D.C.: U.S. Conference of Mayors, no date), pp. 85–86.

command because of the laws and clauses, management's strength in bargaining, budgetary limitations, and the unions' own priorities of interests. They nibble (if not bite) at management prerogatives as they can see opportunities to make the work less arduous, dangerous, and uncomfortable.

How Much Personnel Administration? It is already clear that unions have made deeper inroads into several functions of public personnel administration than into program policy determination, work assignment, and supervision. Some have demanded that more personnel policy matters be negotiable. For example:

AFSCME has demanded, under the [Los Angeles] county ordinance, to negotiate such items as working out of classification, hiring, promotions, discharge, discipline, training, seniority, transfers, probationary period and other issues.

"The right to have an equal voice in setting Civil Service policy involves some 60,000 Los Angeles County employees . . . ," Fiering [the AFSCME council director] said, "It must not be allowed to deteriorate further into a political spoils system beyond the reach of government employees and their bona fide collective bargaining organizations."

Nesvig [the county personnel director] has refused to bargain on issues which he claims are covered by civil service regulations.[9]

Unions have won without difficulty bargained grievance procedures ending in arbitration. They have made impressive gains in establishing collective bargaining as a means of determining pay and benefits and in increasing both. They have started to influence promotions and training, and they have won acceptance for the agency shop in a growing number of localities. However, a deeper penetration, whose components might include a mandatory union shop, bargaining on all job evaluation matters, or establishment of seniority as the basis for promotions to supervisory jobs, is unlikely now. It is prevented by the civil service provisions of charters and laws, by management's resistance to bargaining, and by the unions' need (thus far) to concentrate on more immediate economic issues. It is not difficult to foresee these limits being overrun by steady and resourceful political effort. No doubt this process will be slowed by conservative elements in state legislatures, by the affection for civil service of civic organizations and editorial writers, and by the efforts of business interests to keep

9. "LA Council 36 Fights on Two Fronts," *The Public Employee*, Vol. 35 (March 1970), p. 3.

down governmental costs. But certainly the unions' share in personnel policymaking will increase.

Administration in a Unionized Future

Local government legislators and administrators in the future will be facing unions that have more members and hence more resources, with tested, competent leadership, and with an urge to expand their influence as well as the more specific gains they secure for their membership. These unions may well enjoy adequate political and general community support. It follows that local government programs will not be managed effectively unless administrators realize this and can deal forcefully, understandingly, and competently with a more strongly unionized work force.

Effective administrators of the future will accept the fact of unionism and will use their energies to build and maintain a sound legal framework for union relations, rather than use chauvinistic, unproductive antiunion tactics. Such a structure requires state and local legislation and rules to govern orderly recognition, representation, negotiation, and impasse resolution.[10]

MANAGEMENT STAFFING FOR UNION RELATIONS

Management should organize and staff itself to deal with employee relations. Since unions will frequently (and properly) want to deal with the top personnel man, ideally the same division will hold responsibility for both union relations *and* civil service. But if this is not feasible, the administrative specialist or unit handling the labor function will need to maintain extremely close communication with those working on classification, pay administration, recruitment, promotion, training, and other personnel functions. In large, heavily unionized cities or counties, a likely step may be the establishment of an office of vice mayor or assistant manager for personnel *and* labor relations. At the other end of the continuum, a small town with a modest full-time, or even a part-time, personnel staff may be able to get by with the aid of labor

10. Wellington and Winter, *The Unions and the Cities,* especially Pt. 2.

relations consultants. They can be effective if they can establish continuity in a series of negotiations and can also work satisfactorily with the administration they serve.

Part-time or not, consultants or regular staff, these specialists need a particular competence in *public* union relations. It is not enough to hire the labor negotiator from the local underwear factory or an industrial relations lecturer from a nearby college. The specialist may be three parts labor man, but he will also have to be two parts political scientist, and two parts financial management expert. He cannot be a stranger to problems of local politics, state-local relations, budget formulation, and revenue raising. And if he knows nothing about civil service, he should be able to listen to people who do know something about it.

MAINTAINING MANAGEMENT SECURITY

Public administrators should do everything possible to maintain fundamental management prerogatives—to sharpen distinctions between what is decided by executives and what is negotiable. This effort is far more difficult than in the private sector for two reasons: (1) It is harder to tell where "management" begins; and (2) employees as an interest group are part of the administrator's constituency and thus can follow political avenues in attaining their goals. The effort will be easier if specific levels of supervisors are labeled as "management," given genuine authority over employees, and kept out of nonsupervisory bargaining units; however, this may not be easy to accomplish.

Management security is as important in government as it is in industry and just as susceptible to being nibbled away. Relationships can be clarified and areas of controversy reduced if management's rights are thoroughly discussed with union leaders and then spelled out in legislation, executive orders, or agreements. As a minimum, such provisions should be consistent with responsible, representative government; that is, the officials elected by the people and those to whom they legally delegate their authority should determine the kinds, level, and quality of public services and the allocation of resources among such services. It follows that management should make the basic initial determinations on program objectives, organization structure, financing and manning levels for programs, and work methods (including new technology). Also, since the quality of work depends on the qualifications and effectiveness of employees, management should have the right to select new employees and to choose employees for promotion to supervisory positions. Civil service policies and standards are part of this management prerogative.

In all of these areas, management officials must insist on their rights to make basic decisions if they are to administer their programs responsibly. This does not mean that employees will be defenseless. Unions will negotiate or file grievances in instances where they can show a clear effect on the employees' work. If jobs are eliminated or downgraded (and these were found to be rare events in the nineteen governments studied), various safeguards exist. Most merit systems provide for efforts to reassign employees, for salary protection in downgradings, and for layoff systems favoring senior employees with civil service tenure. Some governments also run out-placement programs to find jobs for employees who are laid off. In addition, unions can bargain (and some have done so) for new salary-saving or job-finding provisions, and for revised lay-off systems.

Another category of management rights is less absolute and more open to union challenge. This group includes the right to classify jobs for pay and other purposes, to administer discipline, to require overtime work, and to assign employees to various locations and shifts. From the management viewpoint these are necessary tools of administration. To the unions, they are working conditions. The extent to which unions may affect them is the result of complex forces: political strengths, bargaining strengths, the vitality of the civil service laws, and, as always, personalities.

A third category of management rights (really, former management rights) are those that are shared and that have become union rights too. These are clearly negotiable, arbitrable matters—pay, hours, fringe benefits, local physical working conditions, and grievance procedures.

Finally, it should be noted again that public officials often miss opportunities to bargain hard and merely use a defensive strategy of responding to union demands. In some units they could bargain for increased productivity, improved work quality, or work rules conducive to efficiency.[11] Such management aggressiveness of course requires skilled work by the union relations staff and high resolution on the part of executives.

LOOKING AHEAD—MORE BILATERALISM IN ADMINISTRATION

The continued sharpening of the distinction between management and employees has been urged here. This is a logical result of the bilateralism fostered by effective unionism. Such a two-party approach also leads to clearer understanding, more specific accountability, and thus more effective administration.

All this does not mean that unions should be ignored in the development of program policies and management policies. Ample opportunities exist at all levels of management for informal consultation or for the use of more structured union-management council meetings to discuss problems of the program or organization. In such discussions—which must be kept separate from bargaining and from the presentation of individual or group grievances—unions can be a productive source of ideas for the solution of urban problems. It is also inevitable that unions will be heard through political channels on policies about which they feel strongly.

The employment transaction between a local government and the citizens who work for it is a more equal bargain, more clearly defined than it was before employees became organized. The increase of unionism in local governments has helped employees to keep up with the rest of the economy and has added to their protection against arbitrary or inconsistent treatment. They have clearly won the rights to organize, to negotiate, and to secure structured consideration of grievances, and they undoubtedly have the right to strike, de facto.[12] But there seems to be little prospect that

11. See discussion of management's bargaining posture in Allan W. Drachman, *Municipal Negotiations: From Differences to Agreement*, No. 5 in series on Strengthening Local Government Through Better Labor Relations (Labor-Management Relations Service of the National League of Cities, U.S. Conference of Mayors, and National Association of Counties, 1970), especially pp. 12, 18–19.

12. For an analysis of the question whether they have this right de jure, see Wellington and Winter, *The Unions and the Cities*. This is also being studied by John F. Burton, Jr., and Arnold R. Weber in their research for this Brookings series.

the transaction will become overbalanced against management, given the continued functioning of the American political system and the exercise by management officials of a reasonable mix of resolution, ability to listen, decisiveness, labor relations knowledge, and good will.

APPENDIX A

Labor Relations Training Programs of the Cities of Detroit and Milwaukee

TABLE A-1. *Labor Relations Training Programs of the Civil Service Commission of the City of Detroit, 1966–69*

Program[a]	Duration	Conducted by	Number enrolled
Courses			
Labor relations for supervisors (general introductory)	12 2-hour sessions	Civil Service Commission training division	350
Labor relations for executives	10 2-hour sessions	Wayne State University	35
Contract administration (general)	5 2-hour sessions	Wayne State University	70
General information session	1 2-hour session	Civil Service Commission training division	1,000
Contract administration	4 2-hour sessions	Civil Service Commission training division	300
Institutes (*special*)			
Institute on negotiations	1 day	Wayne State University	27
Labor relations institute	1 day	Michigan Municipal League	4
Workshops			
Labor relations	2 days	University of Michigan	2
Labor relations	2 days	Public Personnel Association	14
Labor relations	2 days	Cornell University	6
Labor relations	2 days	Wayne State University	20

Source: City of Detroit, Civil Service Commission.

a. The bureau of labor relations of the City of Detroit also distributed to the 3,000 supervisors in the government a "how-to" booklet by Al Leggat and Joseph P. McNamara entitled "Your Blueprint for Day-to-Day Dealings with the Union" (City of Detroit, Labor Relations Bureau, no date; processed).

153

TABLE A-2. *Labor Relations Training Programs of the City Service Commission of the City of Milwaukee, 1964–69*

Year	Program[a]	Hours	Conducted by	Number enrolled
	Courses			
1964	Introduction to labor relations	3	University of Wisconsin instructor	429
1965	Contract administration—train-the-trainer program	6	City Service Commission training unit	28
1966	Contract administration—train-the-trainer program	2	City Service Commission training unit	27
1966	Contract administration for department heads	2	City Service Commission training unit	49
1967	Contract administration—train-the-trainer program	3	City Service Commission training unit	27
1968	1968 labor relations and labor-management relations	2	Consultant	328
1968	Basic labor relations	6	City Service Commission training unit	88
1969	Contract administration	2	City Service Commission training unit	21
1969	Basic labor relations	6	City Service Commission training unit	324
	Institutes, conferences, and other			
1964	Conference on labor relations		National Association of State Labor Relations Agencies	1
1964	Institute on municipal employee relations		University of Wisconsin	2
1964	Arbitration institute		University of Wisconsin	3
1964	Arbitration panel		University of Wisconsin	2
1965	Guide to successful collective bargaining		University of Wisconsin	5
1965	Municipal labor negotiations		Wisconsin and Illinois City Managers	1
1965	Collective bargaining in public employment and fact finding under Wisconsin law		University of Wisconsin	5

TABLE A-2 *Continued*

Year	Program[a]	Conducted by	Number enrolled
	Institutes, conferences, and other (cont.)		
1965	Arbitration panel	University of Wisconsin	2
1965	Public employment and collective bargaining	Public Personnel Association	3
1966	Conference on labor relations training	American Society for Training and Development (Wisconsin chapter)	1
1966	Collective bargaining in the public service	Public Personnel Association	4
1966	Evaluating labor contract costs	University of Wisconsin	1
1966	Collective bargaining in the public service	Industrial Relations Research Association	12
1966	Conference on public employment and collective bargaining	Public Personnel Association	1
1967	Seminar on labor negotiations	Wisconsin League of Municipalities	2
1967	Latest developments in the field of labor negotiations	National Labor Relations Board	5
1968	Bargaining on employee benefits	University of Wisconsin	1
1968	Labor relations for foremen	University of Michigan	1
1968	Labor relations conference	University of Wisconsin	1
1968	Conference on collective bargaining	Public Personnel Association	1
1968	Labor relations seminar	University of Wisconsin	3
1969	International task force on labor relations	International City Managers Association	1
1969	Labor relations in local government	University of Wisconsin	5

Source: City of Milwaukee, City Service Commission.

a. The Milwaukee City Service Commission distributes the following publications for labor relations training purposes: *The Gripevine,* published by the Milwaukee City Service Commission, Administration Division; *Employee Relations in Action,* published by Man and Manager, Inc., New York, N.Y.; *Supervision,* published by National Research Bureau, Inc., Burlington, Iowa; and "Supervisor's Planning Guide," published by Dartnell, Inc., Chicago, Ill.

Pay and Benefit Liberalizations in the Nineteen Local Governments Surveyed

Overtime Pay, Callback Compensation, and Shift Differentials

Recent examples of changes in overtime pay, minimum callback compensation, and shift differentials attributable to bargaining or other union pressures are presented in simplified form below. They vary by bargaining units, by categories of employees, and by dates.

BINGHAMTON

Double time and a half for holidays worked.
Callback: 4 hours minimum at time and a half.

BOSTON

Time and a half for overtime for police. (Other employees had this already.)
Compensatory time off for holidays falling on Saturdays.
$15 a week night shift differential for police.

BUFFALO

Cash (instead of compensatory time off) for overtime.
Cash for holidays worked by policemen.
Callback: 4 hours minimum at straight time.

CINCINNATI

Policemen and firemen: time and a half for overtime; compensatory time off for holidays.
Double time for holidays.

156

Shift differentials: 5 cents an hour for second shift and 10 cents an hour for third shift, increased to 10 cents and 15 cents, respectively.

DADE COUNTY

Night shift differentials liberalized.
Callback time for fire fighters.
5 percent differential for driver-engineer pay (fire fighters).

DAYTON

Cash for overtime for all employees, including police.
10 cents an hour differential for police on night shift.

DETROIT

Callback: 4 hour minimum at overtime rate appropriate for the day; 2 hour minimum for police.
Shift differentials for hospital nurses increased to 40 cents an hour in 1967, 65 cents in 1968, and 70 cents in 1969.

HARTFORD

Overtime:
—For police, time and a half after 44 hours.
—For other employees in bargaining unit, time and a half after 40 hours.
—For nonbargaining unit employees, 5 percent salary differential plus straight time for most blue-collar and clerical supervisors; 5 percent differential plus flexible schedule in lieu of overtime pay for professionals and most middle management and above supervisors.

LOS ANGELES COUNTY

Overtime pay extended to deputy sheriffs and firemen.
Increases in shift differentials: registered nurses, 0 to 35 cents an hour, then 35 cents to 40 cents; vocational nurses, 20 cents to 25 cents; clinical laboratory technologists, 15 cents to 35 cents.

MILWAUKEE

Time and a half for fire fighters after 55 hours.
Straight time for police after 40 hours, and time and a half after 12 hours of overtime in any given two-week pay period.
Time and a half for engineers and technicians at all levels after 40 hours. (Previously there was some unpaid overtime at the higher levels.)
Time and a half in cash for nurses instead of compensatory time off.

Increase in shift differential of 2 cents an hour in 1969 and 2 cents in 1970, except for fire and police, who do not receive shift differential.

MULTNOMAH COUNTY

Cash instead of compensatory time off for overtime.
10 and 15 cents an hour differentials for second and third shifts.

NEW CASTLE COUNTY

Time and a half in cash for overtime.
15 percent night shift differential.
Callback: 4 hours minimum.

NEW ORLEANS

No liberalizations attributable to union activity.

NEW YORK

Successive annual changes: compensatory time off; to cash for straight time; to time and a quarter; to time and a half.
Police: from compensatory time and a half to time and a half paid in cash.
Night shift differentials of 5 percent; nurses aides, 8 percent.

PHILADELPHIA

Higher paid employees made eligible for overtime pay.
Shift differentials doubled: second, 5 cents an hour to 10 cents; third, 10 cents an hour to 20.

ST. LOUIS

10 percent night shift differential.

SAN FRANCISCO

10 percent shift differentials for nurses.

TACOMA

No liberalizations attributable to union activity.

WILMINGTON

Instead of compensatory time off, cash at time and a half, and at double time for Sundays and holidays.
Callback: 4 hours minimum at time and a half.
Shift differentials: second, 10 cents an hour; third, 15 cents.

Annual Leave

Recent instances of increased vacations granted, after union pressure, in some of the cities and counties studied include:

CINCINNATI

4 weeks, 4 days after 15 years.

DAYTON

4 weeks after 20 years;
6 weeks after every 5 years.[1]

LOS ANGELES

3 weeks after 5 years, plus 1 additional day for every year of service to a 20-day maximum.

MILWAUKEE

3 weeks after 8 years.

MULTNOMAH COUNTY *(AFSCME employees only)*

3 weeks after 10 years;
4 weeks after 20 years.

NEW CASTLE COUNTY

3 weeks after 4 years;
4 weeks after 9 years.

SAN FRANCISCO

4 weeks after 15 years.

WILMINGTON

3 weeks after 10 years;
4 weeks after 15 years.

Personal Leave

Unions have also demanded that extra leave for personal purposes be granted or increased. Employees in Buffalo, for example, gave up two religious holidays but gained 5 days of personal leave. Those in Milwaukee were also given an additional day off in 1969 instead of two "lesser holidays." Philadelphia and Binghamton grant three days of

1. The maximum vacation that can be taken in any one year is 22 days, except that every five years 30 days may be taken with the permission of the department head.

what the former calls "administrative leave," and the latter, "personal leave." The city management in Hartford, realizing that policemen were using sick leave for other personal purposes, bargained for a change that discourages this practice. Policemen now receive a bonus of 1 day of personal leave for every 4 months of perfect attendance. Finally, three of the cities studied recently provided for special leave at times of the death of a close relative of an employee. Boston allows up to 3 days' "bereavement leave"; Detroit, 1 to 3; Cincinnati provides 1 day of funeral leave but guards against abuse by limiting such grants to five days in any one year.

Group Life Insurance

Liberalizations occurred in this area too. The union agreement in Dayton called for the city to pay for $3,000 of coverage in 1968, $4,000 in 1969, and $5,000 in 1970. Milwaukee financed $7,000 in 1969 and $8,000 in 1970. Hartford, which provides insurance protection equal to 1.5 times the employee's annual salary, will now pay the full premium cost instead of one-third of it as formerly.[2] Wilmington pays for $3,000, an increase from $1,000. Los Angeles pays for $2,000 and allows the employee to buy more, up to twice his annual salary. Philadelphia, already providing $2,500 of insurance, has extended this benefit to retirees, while New Castle County pays the full premium for life insurance in the amount of half the employee's annual salary.

Retirement

St. Louis eliminated a 6-month waiting period for entry into its retirement system, increased its death benefits, lowered the optional retirement age, and boosted the annuity formula. Cincinnati also raised its annuity formula and made death benefits available to previously ineligible retirees. Milwaukee, which includes elected employee representatives on its pension board, liberalized pension provisions, and increased the city's contribution by an additional 5.5 percent of salary. The pension program is now fully paid for by the city. Both Philadelphia and San Francisco eliminated provisions that reduced a retiree's pension by part of his social security annuity and also increased the city annuities. Finally, New York revised its system to use higher base salaries as well as a more generous formula for annuity computation.

2. For the American Federation of State, County, and Municipal Employees' general employee contract. Provisions differ in the police and fire agreements.

Provisions Relating to Working Conditions of the 1967 Contract between the New York City Department of Social Services and the Social Service Employees Union

1. The City agrees to provide adequate, clean, well-ventilated, safe and sanitary office space, in full compliance with all applicable law and the rules and regulations of the Departments of Health, Buildings, Fire, Labor, and Water Supply, Gas and Electricity, for each employee covered by this contract.

2. The City shall provide each employee covered by this contract with supplies, equipment and telephone services, adequate to perform his duties and responsibilities.

3. All new Social Service Centers shall be air-conditioned. All old Social Service Centers, not yet air-conditioned, shall be converted to air-conditioned status as soon as possible.

4. The City shall permit operation of a vending machine by a concessionaire to make available lunch, coffee and soft drinks on the premises, subject to approval of the Board of Estimate, and to rules and regulations governing use of such machines.

5. **New Locations**—The City agrees to acquire space and open new work locations necessary to comply with all provisions of this contract. The City further agrees to continue to expand the staff [o]f the Bureau of Plant Management on an as-needed basis during the term of this contract. If sufficient qualified staff cannot be recruited, the City agrees to contract out necessary work functions to reduce delays in the establishment of new work locations and additional work space.

6. **Painting**—The City agrees to paint each work location at least once every five (5) years.

161

7. **Lounges**—A lounge area which is usable as a lounge shall be made available in each work location, unless by agreement of the parties such space is temporarily utilized for caseload contract compliance.

8. **Desks and Chairs**—Each Caseworker and Home Economist shall be provided with a desk and chair.

9. **Dictating Machines**—The Department will provide two dictating machines to each three case units plus a 10% reserve of dictating machines in each Social Service Center and Bureau of Child Welfare. These machines shall be kept in good working order. Each dictating machine shall be placed in a sound proof booth. The Division of Day Care shall be provided with a minimum of fifteen (15) new machines. Field Caseworkers in the Division of Day Care shall be permitted to use dictating machines in Social Service Centers, provided the transcription is done at the Division of Day Care.

10. **Adding Machines**—Each Home Economist shall be provided with an adding machine.

11. **Duplicating Machine**—A duplicating machine shall be made available in each Social Service Center, Bureau of Child Welfare location, and the Homemaking Center.

12. **Manuals and Handbooks**—Upon appointment to staff, each employee shall be supplied with a current copy of the appropriate Department of Social Service manual, handbook, and if assigned to field work, a field book.

13. **Coat Racks**—Coat and hat racks for hanging such garments shall be provided on each floor in each work location.

14. **Thermometers**—A thermometer shall be installed on each floor in each work location.

15. **Water Fountains**—Adequate water fountains shall be provided on each floor in each work location, provided that no fountain need be placed on a floor where less than twenty (20) employees are assigned.

16. **Homemaker's Equipment**—Homemakers shall be supplied with the equipment necessary to the performance of their duties including rubber gloves, a sewing kit and a utility bag.

17. **Conference Rooms**—A conference room shall be provided in each Social Service Center, Bureau of Child Welfare location and Homemaking Center; unless by agreement of the parties, such space is temporarily utilized for caseload contract compliance.

18. **Children's Counselors Office Space**—Sufficient office space with desks and chairs shall be provided for Children's Counselors to do required office work.

19. **Centrex**—All new Social Service Centers shall be equipped with a centrex telephone system, and all old Social Service Centers, not yet

equipped with centrex shall be converted, in accordance with schedules to be worked out with the New York Telephone Company. Where centrex cannot be installed in 1967, additional telephones as needed will be provided.

20. **Lockers**—In the planning of new or renovated Children's Centers, lockable clothing lockers shall be provided for Children's Counselors on the basis of one locker per Children's Counselor.

Pending the provision of clothing lockers, the Department agrees to provide a small "valuables" locker for each Children's Counselor.

Source: Article VIII ("Physical Plant, Facilities, Supplies and Equipment") of the contract between the City of New York and the Department of Social Services and the Social Service Employees Union, Sept. 21, 1967.

APPENDIX D

Selected Bibliography

1. *Labor Relations in the Public Service—General*

Advisory Commission on Intergovernmental Relations. *Labor-Management Policies for State and Local Government.* Washington: ACIR, 1969.

Anderson, Arvid. "Public Employee Bargaining." *The Urban Lawyer,* Vol. 1 (Fall 1969).

Begin, James P. "The Development and Operation of Grievance Procedures in Public Employment." Ph.D. dissertation, Purdue University, 1969.

Crouch, Winston W. "The American City and Its Organized Employees," *Urban Data Service,* Vol. 1 (March 1969).

Drachman, Allan W. *Municipal Negotiations: From Differences to Agreement.* No. 5 in series on Strengthening Local Government Through Better Labor Relations. Washington: Labor-Management Relations Service of the National League of Cities, United States Conference of Mayors, and National Association of Counties, 1970.

Godine, Morton R. *The Labor Problem in the Public Service: A Study in Political Pluralism.* Cambridge: Harvard University Press, 1951.

Hanslowe, Kurt L. *The Emerging Law of Labor Relations in Public Employment.* New York State School of Industrial and Labor Relations, Cornell University, 1967.

Hart, Wilson R. *Collective Bargaining in the Federal Civil Service: A Study of Labor-Management Relations in U.S. Government Employment.* New York: Harper, 1961.

Nigro, Felix A. "The Implications for Public Administration," in a symposium on collective negotiations in the public service, *Public Administration Review,* Vol. 28 (March/April 1968).

164

Ross, David B. "The Arbitration of Public Employee Wage Disputes," *Industrial and Labor Relations Review,* Vol. 23 (October 1969).

Spero, Sterling D. *Government as Employer.* New York: Remsen Press, 1948.

Stieber, Jack. "Employee Representation in Municipal Government," in *The Municipal Year Book, 1969.* Washington: The International City Management Association, 1969.

Ullman, Joseph C., and James P. Begin. "The Structure and Scope of Appeals Procedures for Public Employees," *Industrial and Labor Relations Review,* Vol. 23 (April 1970).

Vosloo, Willem B. *Collective Bargaining in the United States Federal Civil Service.* Chicago: Public Personnel Association, 1966.

Wellington, Harry H., and Ralph K. Winter, Jr. "The Limits of Collective Bargaining in Public Employment," *Yale Law Journal,* Vol. 78 (June 1969).

——— ———. *The Unions and the Cities.* Washington: Brookings Institution, 1971.

2. *Power of Public Employee Unions, with Special Reference to Impasses and Strikes*

Banfield, Edward C., and James Q. Wilson. *City Politics.* Cambridge: Harvard University Press, 1963. Chap. 15.

Burton, John F., Jr., and Charles Krider. "The Role and Consequences of Strikes by Public Employees." *Yale Law Journal,* Vol. 79 (January 1970).

Capozzola, John M. "A Growing Militancy," *National Civic Review,* Vol. 58 (June 1969).

Heisel, W. Donald. "Anatomy of a Strike," *Public Personnel Review,* Vol. 30 (October 1969).

Raskin, A. H. "The Revolt of the Civil Servants," *Saturday Review,* Vol. 51 (Dec. 7, 1968).

Stutz, Robert L. "The Resolution of Impasses in the Public Sector," *The Urban Lawyer,* Vol. 1 (Fall 1969).

White, Leonard D. "Strikes in the Public Service," *Public Personnel Review,* Vol. 10 (January 1949).

3. *State Laws on Public Employee Relations*

National Governors Conference, 1967 Executive Committee. *Report of*

Task Force on State and Local Government Labor Relations. Chicago: Public Personnel Association, 1967.

National Governors Conference, Committee on Manpower and Labor Relations. *1968 Supplement to Report of Task Force on State and Local Government Labor Relations.* Chicago: Public Personnel Association, 1968.

National Governors Conference, Committee on Executive Management and Fiscal Affairs. *1969 Supplement to Report of Task Force on State and Local Government Labor Relations.* Chicago: Public Personnel Association, 1969.

Roberts, Harold S. *Labor-Management Relations in the Public Service.* Honolulu: University of Hawaii, Industrial Relations Center, 1968.

4. Labor Relations Primarily in the Private Sector

Armstrong, Richard. "Labor 1970: Angry, Aggressive, Acquisitive," *Fortune,* Vol. 80 (October 1969).

Baer, Walter E. "Subcontracting—Twilight Zone in the Management Function," *Labor Law Journal,* Vol. 16 (October 1965).

Chamberlain, Neil W., and James W. Kuhn. *Collective Bargaining.* 2nd ed. New York: McGraw-Hill, 1965.

Chandler, Margaret K. *Management Rights and Union Interests.* New York: McGraw-Hill, 1964.

Killingsworth, Charles C. "The Presidential Address: Management Rights Revisited," *Arbitration and Social Change: Proceedings of the 22nd Annual Meeting, National Academy of Arbitrators.* Washington: Bureau of National Affairs, 1970.

Kuhn, Alfred. *Labor: Institutions and Economics.* Rev. ed. New York: Harcourt, Brace & World, 1967.

Levine, Marvin J. "Subcontracting—Rights and Restrictions," *Personnel,* Vol. 44 (May–June 1967).

Slichter, Sumner H., James J. Healy, and E. Robert Livernash. *The Impact of Collective Bargaining on Management.* Washington: Brookings Institution, 1960.

5. Public Administration

Charlesworth, James C. (ed.). *Theory and Practice of Public Administration: Scope, Objectives, and Methods.* Philadelphia: American Academy of Political and Social Science, 1968.

Corson, John J., and Joseph P. Harris. *Public Administration in Modern Society.* New York: McGraw-Hill, 1963.

Sayre, Wallace S. "Premises of Public Administration: Past and Emerging," *Public Administration Review,* Vol. 18 (Spring 1958).

6. State and Local Government

Adrian, Charles R. "Governing Megacentropolis: The Politics," *Public Administration Review,* Vol. 30 (September/October 1970).

Fesler, James W. (ed.). *The 50 States and Their Local Governments.* New York: Alfred A. Knopf, 1967.

Sayre, Wallace S., and Herbert Kaufman. *Governing New York City.* New York: Russell Sage Foundation, 1960.

Zimmerman, Joseph F. *State and Local Government.* New York: Barnes & Noble, 1962.

7. Civil Service, Merit Systems, and Public Employment

Advisory Committee on Merit System Standards. *Progress in Intergovernmental Personnel Relations.* Joint publication of U.S. Department of Health, Education, and Welfare; U.S. Department of Defense; and U.S. Department of Labor. Washington: Government Printing Office, 1969.

Dicks, Robert H. "Public Employment and the Disadvantaged: A Close, Hard Look at Testing," *Good Government,* Vol. 86 (Winter 1969).

Dotson, Arch. "The Emerging Doctrine of Privilege in Public Employment," *Public Administration Review,* Vol. 15 (Spring 1955).

———. "A General Theory of Public Employment," *Public Administration Review,* Vol. 16 (Summer 1956).

Logan, Arnold E., and Robert C. Garnier. "Milwaukee's Visual Organizational Inventory," *Public Personnel Review,* Vol. 28 (July 1967).

Rosenbloom, David H. "Citizenship Rights and Civil Service: An Old Issue in a New Phase," *Public Personnel Review,* Vol. 31 (July 1970).

Saunders, Charles B., Jr. *Upgrading the American Police: Education and Training for Better Law Enforcement.* Washington: Brookings Institution, 1970.

Scheuer, William. "Performance Testing in New Jersey," *Good Government,* Vol. 87 (Spring 1970).

Stahl, O. Glenn. *Public Personnel Administration.* 6th ed. New York: Harper & Row, 1971.

8. Salaries and Fringe Benefits

Danielson, William F. "Why Pay Policemen and Firemen the Same Salary?" *Public Personnel Review,* Vol. 25 (July 1964).

Garnier, Robert C., and William Snell. "Management Pay in Milwaukee," *Public Personnel Review,* Vol. 31 (July 1970).

Grant, Robert J., and Paul Saenz. "The Police/Fire Parity Issue," *The Police Chief,* Vol. 35 (September 1968).

Lutz, Carl F. "Overcoming Obstacles to Professionalism," *The Police Chief,* Vol. 35 (September 1968).

———. "Relating Police and Fire Department Salaries," Personnel Brief 33. Public Personnel Association, no date; processed.

Perry, George L. *Unemployment, Money Wage Rates, and Inflation.* Cambridge: M.I.T. Press, 1966.

Strasser, Arnold. "Police and Firemen's Salary Trends," *Monthly Labor Review,* Vol. 92 (August 1969).

Talbot, Joseph E., Jr. "An Analysis of Changes in Wages and Benefits During 1969," *Monthly Labor Review,* Vol. 93 (June 1970).

9. Fiscal Problems of Local Governments

Advisory Commission on Intergovernmental Relations. *Fiscal Balance in the American Federal System.* Washington: ACIR, 1967. 2 vols.

———. *State Aid to Local Government.* Washington: ACIR, 1969.

———. *State and Local Finances: Significant Features, 1967 to 1970.* Washington: ACIR, 1969.

Bahl, Roy W. "State Taxes, Expenditures and the Fiscal Plight of the Cities," in Alan K. Campbell (ed.). *The States and the Urban Crisis.* Englewood Cliffs: Prentice-Hall, 1970.

Bernstein, David. "Financing the City Government," in *Governing the City: Challenges and Options for New York.* New York: Academy of Political Science, 1969.

Bradford, D. F., R. A. Malt, and W. E. Oates, "The Rising Cost of Local Public Services: Some Evidence and Reflections," *National Tax Journal,* Vol. 22 (June 1969).

Committee for Economic Development. *Fiscal Issues in the Future of Federalism.* Supplementary Paper No. 23. New York, 1968.

Ecker-Racz, L. L. *The Politics and Economics of State-Local Finance.* Englewood Cliffs: Prentice-Hall, 1970.

———. "New Directions in Intergovernmental Fiscal Relations," *Minnesota Municipalities* (September 1969).

"Financing Our Urban Needs$$," *Nation's Cities,* Vol. 7 (March 1969).

Harriss, C. Lowell. *Handbook of State and Local Government Finance.* New York: Tax Foundation, 1966.

Levy, Michael E. "Sharing Federal Revenue with the States: A Comparison of the ACIR and Nixon Proposals," *The Conference Board Record,* Vol. 7 (April 1970).

Manvel, Allen D. *Urban America and the Federal System.* Washington: Advisory Commission on Intergovernmental Relations, 1969. (Especially Chapter 2, "Restoring Fiscal Balance in the Federal System.")

Netzer, Dick. "The Budget: Trends and Prospects," in Lyle C. Fitch and Annmarie Hauck Walsh (eds.). *Agenda for a City.* Beverly Hills: Sage Publications, 1970.

Pechman, Joseph A. "The Rich, the Poor, and the Taxes They Pay," *The Public Interest* (Fall 1969) (Brookings Reprint 168).

Perloff, Harvey S., and Richard P. Nathan (eds.). *Revenue Sharing and the City.* Baltimore: The Johns Hopkins Press, 1968.

Revenue Sharing and Its Alternatives: What Future for Fiscal Federalism? Hearings before the Subcommittee on Fiscal Policy of the Joint Economic Committee, 90 Cong. 1 sess. Washington: Government Printing Office, 1967.

Shannon, John. "Financing Urban America—Time for a Change," *Municipal Finance* (August 1969).

10. Budgeting in the Public Service

Brenman, Edwin. "Budgeting: How It's Done in the Nation's Largest City," *Public Management,* Vol. 51 (August 1969).

Burkhead, Jesse. *Government Budgeting.* New York: John Wiley & Sons, 1956.

Crecine, John P. "A Computer Simulation Model of Municipal Budgeting," *Management Science,* Vol. 13 (July 1967).

Mushkin, Selma J. "PPBS in City, State, and County: An Overview," in *Innovations in Planning, Programing, and Budgeting in State and Local Governments.* A Compendium of Papers Submitted to the Subcommittee on Economy in Government of the Joint Economic

Committee, 91 Cong. 1 sess. 1969. Washington: Government Printing Office, 1969.

Pois, Joseph. "Personnel Implications of New York City's Budget Process," in David T. Stanley, *Professional Personnel for the City of New York*. Washington: Brookings Institution, 1963.

Schick, Allen. "Control Patterns in State Budget Execution," *Public Administration Review*, Vol. 24 (June 1964).

"A Symposium—Planning-Programming-Budgeting System Reexamined: Development, Analysis, and Criticism," *Public Administration Review*, Vol. 29 (March/April 1969).

Index

Administrative officer: government role, 7–9

Adrian, Charles R., 144*n*

Advisory Committee on Intergovernmental Relations, 10, 114

Affiliated unions, *see* Unions

AFSCME, *see* American Federation of State, County, and Municipal Employees

American Arbitration Association, 53

American Federation of State, County, and Municipal Employees (AFSCME), 2; budget role, 122; and civil service, 34, 37; contracting-out, 92; employee training, 47; fringe benefits, 87; management rights, 23–24; manning influence, 100; membership, 137; out-of-title work, 63; overtime, 81; pay-setting, 66, 68; promotion policy, 39, 41, 43–44, 47; strike use, 122–23; strength of, 13, 137

Anderson, Arvid, 145, 146*n*

Antipoverty programs, 47–49

Appointing officer (civil service), 8, 35, 38

Arbitration: in budget process, 132; costs, 53; in grievance procedure, 52–53; "third party," 50, 52; volume, 55

Armstrong, Richard, 75*n*

Baer, Walter E., 91*n*

Baldinger, Wilbur H., 146*n*

Bales, Carter F., 119*n*

Banfield, Edward C., 137

Bargaining responsibility, 20–21, 25–29. *See also* Unions

Begin, James P., 50, 51*n*, 52, 54

Bernstein, David, 127*n*

Binghamton: bargaining responsibility, 27; budget process, 116; contracting-out, 91; government form, 7; grievance procedure, 52*n*, 55; management rights, 22*n*; merit system, 9; out-of-title work, 63; pay-setting, 71; working conditions, 107–08

"Blue flu" strikes, 3, 68, 78

Board of Supervisors: Los Angeles County, 8; San Francisco, 8, 125

Boston: bargaining responsibility, 27; budget process, 117; contracting-out, 92; employee training, 47; fringe benefits, 85; government form, 7–8; grievance procedure, 52*n;* hours of work, 80; merit system, 9; out-of-title work, 106; pay-setting, 73; promotion policy, 42; union shop in, 14; working conditions, 108

Boston City Hospital, 48

Brenman, Edwin, 119*n*

Budget, city: arbitration panels, 132; collective bargaining, 115–18; controls, 133–35; Emergency Aid for Cities program, 127; fact-finding panels, 131–32; "forced accruals," 134; growth, 123–31; PPBS use, 119–20; preparation, 115–20; reserves, 118–19; revenue sources, 113–15, 121–23, 125–32; state aid, 114, 127–28; union influence, 112, 121–23, 140–41

Budget directors: bargaining, 27

Buffalo: budget process, 116, 119, 121, 130, 133; contracting-out, 92; fringe benefits, 86; government form, 7; management rights, 22*n*; out-of-title work, 63, 106; overtime, 102; pay-setting, 66;

public employee relations board, 12; work location, 104

Burkhead, Jesse, 133*n*

Burnham, David, 86*n*

Burton, John F., Jr., 18*n*, 65*n*, 78*n*, 91*n*, 144*n*, 151*n*

California: collective bargaining law, 11–12

California Association of Professional Employees: contracting-out, 92

Carroll, Maurice, 98*n*, 104

Central Labor Council (New York), 2

Chamberlain, Neil W., 16*n*, 17*n*, 89*n*

Chandler, Margaret K., 91*n*

Charlesworth, James C., 4*n*

Cincinnati: arbitration, 53*n*; budget process, 119, 122–23; collective bargaining, 12; council-manager government, 8; employee training, 47; fringe benefits, 85, 124; grievances, 52; management rights, 23; merit system, 9, 12; out-of-title work, 64, 106; pay-setting, 66, 69, 78, 122–24; promotion policy, 41, 47; working conditions, 107–08

City government: collective bargaining role, 11–13, 25–30; forms of, 7–8; pay-setting policy, 73–74; union influence, 58–59, 86–87, 138–40. *See also* Budget; Management; specific city

Civil service, 9–10, 19, 32–45, 50; and antipoverty programs, 48–49; classification role, 61–62; effect of unionism, 32–45; examination, 34–35; exemptions, 9; federal standard, 10; grievance procedure, 51, 55; out-of-title work, 63–64; and supervisors, 45; union attitude, 37, 141, 147; state "mandating," 10

Civil service associations, 14

Classification plan: and civil service, 61–62; definition, 60–61; higher titles, 62; management rights, 150; out-of-title work, 63–64; re-evaluation, 61–62; union attitude, 61

Cleveland Metropolitan General Hospital, 48

Clothing allowances, 109

Collective bargaining: bilateral nature, 30–31, 101; in budget process, 115–18; department head role, 28–29; illegal delegation of power doctrine, 18; local options, 11–13; management responsibility, 25–30; "memoranda of understanding," 11–12; pay-setting, 65–73; politics of, 19; public-private compari-

son, 19–20; sovereignty doctrine, 17–18; state statutes, 10–13; training need, 29–30

Committee on Political Education (Philadelphia), 2

Connecticut: collective bargaining law, 11–12

Contracting-out: anti-contracting policy, 92, 111; and management rights clauses, 24

Cornell School of Industrial and Labor Relations, 30

Corson, John J., 4*n*

Council-manager government, 7–8

County government: types, 8–9. *See also* specific county

Crecine, John P., 115*n*

Crouch, Winston W., 13*n*

Dade County: bargaining responsibility, 29; budget process, 117, 125–28; contracting-out, 92; employee training, 46; fringe benefits, 84, 86; garbage collectors' strike, 3; government form, 8; grievance procedure, 52*n*; hazard pay, 82; management rights, 22*n*; manning problem, 97; merit system, 9; out-of-title work, 64, 105–06; pay-setting, 71, 73, 79, 125–28; probation periods, 35; promotion policy, 40–42; shift assignment, 103; training, in labor relations, 30; work location, 105; working conditions, 108

Danielson, William F., 69*n*

Dayton: agency shop agreement, 14*n*; bargaining responsibility, 12, 27, 29; budget process, 117, 128–29; council-manager government, 8; employee training, 46; fringe benefits, 84–85; grievance procedure, 52*n*, 54–55; management rights, 23; pay-setting, 66, 72, 128–29; promotion policy, 33, 37, 40, 41; work location, 105

Dayton Public Service Union: hiring practices, 33; management rights clauses, 23; pay-setting, 66, 72

Delaware: collective bargaining law, 11–12; fringe benefit statute, 85

Delaware, University of, 30

Dental care, 87. *See also* Fringe benefits

Department head: budget role, 115, 133; collective bargaining role, 28–30; union influence, 141–42

Detroit: agency shop agreement, 14*n*; antipoverty programs, 49; bargaining responsibility, 27, 29; budget process, 116, 125–27, 133; classification plan, 62; contracting-out, 92; discipline process, 56; employee training, 46–47; fringe benefits, 84–85, 87; government form, 7; grievance procedure, 51, 52n, 54; hours of work, 80; manning problem, 100; merit system, 9–10; pay-setting, 67–68, 72n, 73, 78–79; police strike, 3; promotion policy, 39, 41–44; training, in labor relations, 30; unions, 13; work location, 104–05; working conditions, 108, 110

Detroit City Hospital Employees Union, 43

Detroit Police Officers' Association, 78

Dicks, Robert H., 34n

Disadvantaged, programs for, 34, 47–49, 137

Discipline process: procedures, 55–56; union attitude, 56, 58

Disease prevention, 108–09

Drachman, Allan W., 151n

Ecker-Racz, L. L., 113n

Education: civil service requirement, 34. *See also* Training

Elected council: council-manager government, 8; mayor government, 7

Emergency Aid for Cities program, 127

Employee: defined, 20–21; rights, 17–20. *See also* Unions

Engineers' associations, 14

Essentiality doctrine: and right to strike, 18

Eye care, 87. *See also* Fringe benefits

Fact-finding panels: in budget process, 131–32

Federal government: and city budget, 114; civil service standard, 10; pay-setting indexes, 71, 74–75

Federal Mediation and Conciliation Service, 53

Fesler, James W., 7n

Firemen: grievance process, 53; hours of work, 79–80; manning problem, 97–98; out-of-title work, 105; overtime, 81; pay-setting, 66, 68–69, 71–73; promotion policy, 38, 41–44; training programs, 46; working conditions, 108. *See also* International Association of Fire Fighters

Fitch, Lyle C., 114n

Florida: collective bargaining law, 11; merit systems, 9n; pay equity statute, 68–69

Fraternal Order of Police, 13, 66. *See also* Police

Fringe benefits, 71–72, 82–87; automobile allowance, 87, 110; health insurance, 84–85; life insurance, 84–85; medical care, 84–87; rest periods, 109–10; retirement, 85–86; sick leave, 84; state statutes, 84–85; union influence, 147; vacations and holidays, 83–84; welfare funds, 86–87

Garment workers: welfare funds, 87

Garnier, Robert C., 21n, 73n

Godine, Morton R., 17n

Government, *see* City government; County government; Federal government; State government; Management

Grant, Robert J., 69n

Gribbs, Roman S.: on hours of work, 80

Grievance procedure: binding arbitration, 52–53; civil service role, 51, 55; cost, 53; out-of-title work, 63–64; overtime, 81; scope, 50–52; steps in, 52–53; union contracts, 50; volume, 54–55

Hanslowe, Kurt L., 17n

Harris, Joseph P., 4n

Hartford: bargaining responsibility, 27, 29; budget process, 116, 119, 133–34; council-manager government, 8; employee training, 46; fringe benefits, 84–85; grievance procedure, 52n; hours of work, 80; management rights, 24; overtime, 81–82, 102; probation periods, 35; training, in labor relations, 30; union shop agreements, 14; work location, 104; working conditions, 108

Hartman, Paul T., 60n, 74n, 99n

Hatch Act, 2n; "little Hatch acts," 2

Haughton, Ronald W., 68n, 79n, 126n

Hawaii, public employee strikes, 3n

Hazard pay, 82

Health insurance, 84–85. *See also* Fringe benefits

Health and safety: manning problem, 97–99; overtime factor, 102; and strikes, 78; working conditions, 107–09

Healy, James J., 40n, 91n

Heisel, W. Donald, 68n, 123n, 124n

Hiring practice: civil service examination, 34–35; merit principle, 33; performance tests, 34; union influence, 32–36

Hours of work, 67, 79–80

IAFF, *see* International Association of Fire Fighters
Illegal delegation of power doctrine, 17
International Association of Fire Fighters (IAFF), 13; manning problem, 97; pay-setting, 66, 69; promotion policy, 40, 43. *See also* Firemen
Interviews, scope of, 15

Kaufman, Herbert, 137
Kihss, Peter, 96n
Killingsworth, Charles C., 24n, 68n, 79n, 126n
Krider, Charles, 18n, 91n
Kuhn, Alfred, 17n; on management rights, 21–22
Kuhn, James W., 16n, 17n, 89n

Laguna Honda Hospital, 54, 56, 102
Levine, Marvin J., 91n
Levy, Michael E., 114n
Life insurance, 84–85. *See also* Fringe benefits
Lindsay, John: on hours of work, 80
"Little Hatch acts," 2
Livernash, E. Robert, 40n, 91n
Location, *see* Work location
Logan, Arnold E., 21n
Los Angeles County: budget process, 117, 130; civil service associations, 14; collective bargaining law, 11–12; contracting-out, 92; discipline process, 56; employee relations commission, 11–13, 22; employee training, 48; government form, 8; grievance procedure, 52n; hazard pay, 82; hospital and social workers' strike, 3; hours of work, 80; management rights, 22n; merit system, 10; out-of-title work, 64; pay-setting, 65; promotion system, 38; SEIU locals, 13; training, in labor relations, 29–30; union security agreements, 14; workload policy, 97
Los Angeles County Employees Association: and discipline process, 56
Louisiana, 11
Lutz, Carl F., 69n

Management: bargaining responsibility, 25–30; budget process, 135; classification role, 150; contracting-out, 90–93; defined, 20–21; employee training, 46–49; grievance procedure role, 52–53; labor relations staff, 29–30, 148–49;

management rights clauses, 23–24, 90, 100, 146; manning problem, 98–101; out-of-title work, 105–07; overtime, 101–02, 150; pay-setting, 64–65; prerogatives, 21–24, 145–51; promotion policy, 36–45; shift assignments, 102–04, 146; union influence, 58–59, 89–90, 138–40; work location, 104–05, 150; working conditions role, 107–11. *See also* City government
Management rights clauses, 22–25, 90, 100, 146
Manager: government role, 8–9
"Mandating": in civil service system, 10
Manning problem: fire fighting, 97–98; management role, 98–101; and safety, 97–99; and technological change, 99–100
Marshall, James, 120n
Massachusetts: collective bargaining law, 11–12
Maternity leave, 87. *See also* Fringe benefits
Meal allowance, 110. *See also* Fringe benefits
Medical care, 84–87. *See also* Fringe benefits
"Memoranda of understanding": in collective bargaining, 11–12; in pay-setting, 65
Merit principle, *see* Civil service
Michigan: collective bargaining law, 11–12
Michigan Nurses Association: promotion policy, 43
Mileage allowance, 110. *See also* Fringe benefits
Milwaukee: bargaining responsibility, 21, 27, 29; budget process, 119, 131; contracting-out, 92; employee training, 47; employment standards, 33; fringe benefits, 84–85; government form, 7–8; grievance procedure, 52n, 54–55; hours of work, 80; merit system, 10; out-of-title work, 63–64, 105; pay-setting, 69–70, 72–73, 79; promotion policy, 38, 41, 42; training, in labor relations, 30; working conditions, 108
Milwaukee County Hospital, 48
Missouri: collective bargaining law, 11–12
Morgenstern, Martin, 94n
Multnomah County: bargaining responsibility, 27; budget process, 133; contracting-out, 92; fringe benefits, 84;

government form, 8–9; management rights, 22*n;* overtime, 102; promotion policy, 37; work location, 104; working conditions, 110

Municipal Improvement League (San Francisco), 2

Mushkin, Selma J., 119*n*

Nathan, Richard P., 114*n*

National League of Cities, 122

Neighborhood Youth Corps, 48–49

Netzer, Dick, 114*n*, 120*n*, 127*n*

New careers program, 34, 48, 96

New Castle County: budget process, 117, 119; employee training, 48; fringe benefits, 85; government form, 9; grievance procedure, 52*n;* management rights, 24; merit system, 9; out-of-title work, 63; overtime, 102; union shop agreements, 14; working conditions, 107

New Orleans: budget process, 117, 130, 133; contracting-out, 91–92; fringe benefits, 84; garbage collectors' strike, 3; government form, 7–8; grievances, 52; hours of work, 80; management rights, 22*n;* merit system, 10; pay-setting, 65; promotion policy, 38, 42; union agreement, 14*n;* work location, 105; working conditions, 108

New York City: antipoverty programs, 49; bargaining responsibility, 11–12, 23, 27, 29; budget process, 113, 117, 127–28, 134; Central Labor Council, 2; classification role, 62; employee training, 46; fringe benefits, 84–87; government form, 7; grievance procedure, 52*n;* hours of work, 80; Housing Authority, 13; management rights, 22–24; manning problem, 97–98; merit system, 9; out-of-title work, 64, 106; pay-setting, 67, 72–73, 79; police strike, 3; promotion system, 37, 39, 42; recreation workers, 34; shift assignment, 103–04; training, in labor relations, 30; Uniformed Fire Fighters, 33; welfare workers, 33, 93–96; work location, 104–05; working conditions, 108, 110; workload problem, 97–98

New York City Board of Collective Bargaining, 23

New York City Housing Authority, 13

New York State: fringe benefits statute, 85–86; public employee relations boards, 12

Nixon, Richard M.: revenue sharing, 114

Nursing associations, 14

Ohio: collective bargaining law, 12–13; fringe benefit statute, 85

Oregon: collective bargaining law, 11; public employee relations boards, 12

Out-of-title work, 63–64, 105–07

Overtime, 80–82, 101–02; management right, 150

Patrolmen's Benevolent Association (New York), 86, 103–04

Pay-setting: bargaining in, 65–73; increases, 75–79; informal, 65; by indexes, 71–72; methods, 64–73; out-of-title work, 63–64; overtime, 80–82; preparations, 65–67; problems, 72–73; and reevaluation classification, 61–62; special arrangements, 80–82; union influence, 64–74, 76–79, 147–48

Pechman, Joseph A., 114*n*

Pennsylvania: collective bargaining law, 11–12; public employee strikes, 3*n*

Pension systems, *see* Retirement

Performance rating: and grievance procedure, 51; promotion policy, 34, 36, 38, 40–41

Performance test: vs. civil service examination, 34

Perloff, Harvey S., 114*n*

Perry, George L., 75*n*

Personnel management: effect of unionism on, 25–31

Phalon, Richard, 113*n*, 122*n*, 128*n*

Philadelphia: antipoverty programs, 49; bargaining responsibility, 27; budget process, 117, 130, 133; Committee on Political Education, 2; employee training, 48; fringe benefits, 84–85; government form, 7–8; grievance procedure, 55; management rights, 22*n;* out-of-title work, 63; overtime, 102; pay-setting, 66; promotion policy, 41–42; union shop agreements, 14; working conditions, 107

Philadelphia General Hospital, 49

Planning, Programming, Budgeting System (PPBS), 119–20

Pois, Joseph, 134*n*

Police: Fraternal Order of Police, 13, 66; grievance procedure, 53; manning problem, 98; out-of-title work, 106; overtime, 81; Patrolmen's Benevolent Association, 86, 103–04; pay-setting, 66, 68–71, 75–79; promotion policy,

38, 41–43; shift assignment, 103–04; training programs, 46; union representation, 13; working conditions, 108

Policy, *see* Program policy

Political power (union), 1–3, 19–20, 136–38

Position classification, *see* Classification plan

PPBS, *see* Planning, Programming, Budgeting System

Probation period: union influence, 35–36

Professionals: and public employee unionism, 14. *See also* Supervisors

Program policy: union influence, 93–96, 146

Promotion: and appointing officer, 38; examination for, 38–41, 44; methods, 40–45; open competition, 37–40; performance rating, 34, 36, 38, 40–41, 44; rule of three, 35–38, 40–42; selection devices, 38–41; and seniority, 41–45; training programs, 47

Public administration: defined, 4–5; politics of, 5; study regions, 5–7. *See also* City government; County government; Management

Public employee relations boards, 12

Public employment relations statutes, 142

Public Personnel Association, 30

Race: in civil service, 34, 137; strike use, 3

Raskin, A. H., 3n, 143n

Rest periods, 109–10. *See also* Fringe benefits

Reston, James, 3n, 143n

Retirement, 85–86. *See also* Fringe benefits

Ross, David B., 132n

Saenz, Paul, 69n

Safety, *see* Health and safety

Salary, *see* Pay-setting

San Francisco: blue-collar craftsmen, 33; budget process, 117, 124–25; civil service associations, 14; fringe benefits, 85; government form, 7–8; hazard pay, 82; hospital workers' strike, 3; hours of work, 80; management rights, 22n; Municipal Improvement League, 2; out-of-title work, 106; pay-setting, 65–66, 69, 71–73, 124–25; probation officer strike, 96–97; promotion policy, 39, 41; SEIU locals, 13, 34; welfare workers, 33

Saunders, Charles B., Jr., 46n

Sayre, Wallace S.: on management power, 137; on public administration, 5

Scheuer, William, 35n

Schick, Allen, 133n

SEIU, *see* Service Employees International Union

Seniority: management practice, 37; overtime, 102; promotion factor, 37, 41–45; shift assignment, 111; work location, 104, 111

Service Employees International Union (SEIU): and contracting-out, 92; employment standards, 34; membership, 13, 137; pay-setting, 66; working conditions, 108

Sewerage and Water Board (New Orleans), 65

Shift assignment, 102–04, 111, 146, 150

Sick leave, 84. *See also* Fringe benefits

Slichter, Sumner H., 40n, 91n

Smith, Russell A., 68n, 79n, 126n

Snell, William, 73n

Social Service Employees Union (SSEU): 1965 strike, 93–96; employee training, 46; hiring practices, 33; management rights clause, 23–24; promotion policy, 42; working conditions, 110

Sovereignty doctrine, 17–18

SSEU, *see* Social Service Employees Union

Stahl, O. Glenn, 34n, 36n

Stanley, David T., 134n

State government: collective bargaining laws, 10–13; merit system role, 10; public employee relations boards, 12; union influence, 142–43

Steiner, Gilbert, Y., 94n

Stieber, Jack, 2n, 13n

St. Louis: budget process, 117, 122, 129–30, 133; collective bargaining, 11; fringe benefits, 84–85; garbage collectors' strike, 3; government form, 7; grievances, 52; hours of work, 80; management rights, 22n; pay-setting, 65, 70, 129–30; union security agreements, 14

Strasser, Arnold, 75n

Strikes: "blue flu," 68, 78; and essentiality doctrine, 18; illegal, 143–44; numbers, 18–19; pay-setting, 78–79; politics of, 3, 19–20, 137; and race use, 3; theory of, 18

Stutz, Robert L., 18n

Supervisors: labor relations training, 29–30; overtime, 82; pay-setting, 72–73; promotion policy, 45; union influence, 56, 58–59

Tacoma: bargaining responsibility, 29; budget, 133; council-manager government, 8; grievances, 52; management rights, 22n; pay-setting, 66; police requirements, 33–34; promotion policy, 37, 41

Talbot, Joseph E., Jr., 72n, 74n

Taxation: income, 113, 125–26, 128–29; property, 113–14, 124–25, 130; sales, 113, 130

Taylor law, 86, 116

Teamsters union: in city governments, 13; contracting-out, 92; employee training, 47; fringe benefits, 86; manning problems, 100; out-of-title work, 63, 106; pay-setting, 68; promotion policy, 39, 43–44, 47; welfare funds, 87; working conditions, 108

Technological change: manning problem, 99–100

"Third party": in grievance procedure, 50, 52

Time period: in out-of-title work, 63

Tolchin, Martin, 99n

Training: antipoverty programs, 47–49; employee, 46–49; for promotion, 47; in labor relations, 29–30; union support, 47, 49

Ullman, Joseph C., 51n

Uniformed Fire Fighters Association (New York), 33

Union security, 14n

United Mine Workers: welfare funds, 87

Unions: affiliated, 13; antipoverty programs, 49; budget process, 112, 115–17, 123–31, 135; city revenue assistance, 121–22; city government effect, 58–59, 89–90; civil service as restraint, 37, 147; classification attitude, 61–62; contracting-out, 90–93, 111; discipline process, 56, 58; and department heads, 141–42; employee training, 46–47; fringe benefits, 87, 147; grievance procedure, 50–54; effect on hiring, 32–36; hours of work issue, 79–80; as interest group, 138; labor solidarity aspect, 137; and management prerogatives, 145–51; management rights clauses, 22–25, 90, 100, 146; manning problem, 97–101; membership, 2, 136; out-of-title work, 63–64, 105–07; overtime pay, 80–82, 101–02; pay-setting, 65–74, 75–79, 147; personnel management organization,

25–31; program policy influence, 146; political power, 1–3, 19–20, 136–38; and probation period, 35–36; promotion influence, 36–45; professionals in, 14, 33–34; restraints on, 143–48; safety interest, 107–09; seniority objectives, 36, 41; shift assignment, 102–04; and state government, 142–43; types of, 13–14; union shop agreements, 14; welfare policy, 87, 146; working conditions, 107–11; workload influence, 93–97. *See also* Strikes

U.S. Bureau of Labor Statistics, 74–75, 83

U.S. Department of Labor: employee training program, 48; pay-setting indexes, 71

Vacation and holidays, 83–84. *See also* Fringe benefits

Vermont, public employee strikes, 3n

Walsh, Annmarie Hauck, 114n

Washington: collective bargaining law, 11–12

Weaver, Warren, Jr., 114n

Weber, Arnold R., 65n, 78n, 144n, 151n

Welfare funds, 86–87

Wellington, Harry H., 11n, 17n, 18n, 51n, 78n, 144n, 148, 151n

White, Leonard D., 18n

Wilmington: bargaining responsibility, 29; employee training, 46; fringe benefits, 85; government form, 7; hours of work, 80; management rights, 22n; out-of-title work, 63; overtime, 102; pay-setting, 66, 73; promotion policy, 42; training, in labor relations, 30; union shop agreements, 14; working conditions, 108

Wilson, James Q., 137

Winter, Ralph K., 11n, 17n, 18n, 51n, 78n, 144n, 148n, 151n

Wisconsin: collective bargaining law, 11–12

Work assignment: locations, 104–05; overtime assignment, 101–02; shift assignment, 102–04

Work Incentive Program, 48

Work location, 104–05, 111, 150

Working conditions: clothing, 109; rest periods, 109–11; safety, 107–09

Workload: union influence, 93–97

Zimmerman, Joseph L., 7n